On Being
a Servant
of God

Other Titles by Warren W. Wiersbe (Selected)

Be Myself
The Bible Exposition Commentary (2 vols.)
The Bumps Are What You Climb On
The Cross of Jesus
Developing a Christian Imagination
Elements of Preaching
God Isn't in a Hurry
The Intercessory Prayer of Jesus
Living with the Giants
The Names of Jesus
Prayer, Praise, and Promises
Preaching and Teaching With Imagination
Real Worship
So That's What a Christian Is!
Turning Mountains into Molehills
Victorious Christians You Should Know
Wiersbe's Expository Outlines on the New Testament
Wiersbe's Expository Outlines on the Old Testament
Windows on the Parables

On Being a Servant of God

Warren W. Wiersbe

Baker Books
A Division of Baker Book House Co.
Grand Rapids, Michigan 49516

© 1993 by Warren W. Wiersbe

Published by Baker Books
a division of Baker Book House Company
P.O. Box 6287, Grand Rapids, MI 49516-6287

First cloth edition published 1993 by Oliver-Nelson Books, a division of Thomas
Nelson Publishers.

First paperback edition published 1999 by Baker Books

Seventh printing, February 2003

Printed in the United States of America

Library of Congress Cataloging-in-Publication Data

Wiersbe, Warren W.
    On being a servant of God / Warren W. Wiersbe.
       p.   cm.
    Originally published: Nashville : T. Nelson, c1993.
    Includes bibliographical references.
    ISBN 0-8010-9086-5 (pbk.)
    1. Church work. I. Title.
  [BV4400.W515   1999]
  248.4—dc21   98-33932

For information about academic books, resources for Christian leaders, and all
new releases available from Baker Book House, visit our web site:
http://www.bakerbooks.com

CONTENTS

Foreword

What a blessed day it was when I received my first copy of *On Being a Servant of God*. Warren Wiersbe has written more than a hundred books, but this one stands out in a unique way. Its simplicity and down-to-earth approach to the basics of Christian service made a deep impact on my heart. His definition of what ministry really is should be memorized and meditated on by every pastor, Christian leader, and believer who wants to serve the Lord.

The author has vast experience as both a pastor and a biblical expositor. He wisely draws from both backgrounds in handling topics that very few have approached with such clarity and insight. These nuggets are extremely valuable for everyone who faces the immense challenge of ministering to people in the name of the Lord Jesus Christ.

I have purchased and distributed more than a hundred copies of *On Being a Servant of God* because I wanted other pastors and friends to benefit from this gem of a book. No one who reads this book with an open and prayerful heart can remain the same. In a day when Christian ministry is attacked and challenged in so many ways, God has provided a wonderful source of wisdom to all who will read and then ask God at the throne of grace to become a true servant of God.

Jim Cymbala
Senior Pastor, The Brooklyn Tabernacle

BY WAY
OF
INTRODUCTION

My heart rejoices to know that God is using this little book to encourage His servants around the world and that another printing is called for, this time from Baker Book House.

This new printing gives me the opportunity to thank the many people who have phoned, written, and faxed, or stopped me at conferences, to express their gratitude for *On Being a Servant of God*. Some have told me they have given copies to local church staff personnel and officers, and that the book has helped them greatly. For this we give thanks and glory to God.

This book is for ministers spelled with a small "m," as well as for those who are in what we call "full-time Christian service." (All of us should be involved in "full-time Christian living.") We're laborers together with the Lord; so whether you are a minister (small "m") or a Minister (capital "M"), there's bound to be some word of help and encouragement for you in these pages. The fact that your paycheck comes from IBM and not First Church doesn't mean you aren't a minister of the Lord.

These thirty chats contain the kind of counsel I wish somebody had shared with me when I began my Christian pilgrimage back in 1945. Christian ministry never has been easy, but it's even more difficult today when the ages are colliding, the boundaries are disappearing, and the definitions are changing. You get the impression that nothing is any longer what it used to be. But the basic principles of Christian service really haven't changed, and that's what I've focused on in these pages.

I hope they encourage and help you.

WARREN W. WIERSBE

P.S. For a more detailed exposition of Christian ministry, see *Ten Power Principles for Christian Service*, which my pastor-son David and I wrote, also published by Baker Book House. It explains and applies ten principles for ministry that will work, no matter what your calling or gifts.

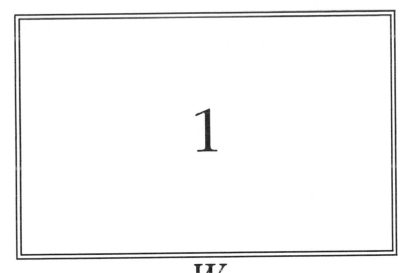

*W*hether you are a volunteer or a full-time Christian worker, I wish I could sit down and leisurely chat with you about your ministry. I obviously can't do that, so I'm doing the next best thing and sharing my thinking with you in this book. Perhaps you're just getting started in your ministry, or you may be a veteran with battle scars. In either case, I trust that what I say will encourage you in the greatest work in the world, serving the Lord Jesus Christ.

Serving God is a wonderful thing if we understand what it is and how God does it through us. Ministering for Jesus Christ can be as uplifting and exciting as hang gliding, or it can be as burdensome and boring as rolling the same rock up the mountain as Sisyphus did in the Greek myth. No matter how difficult the work or how many times we feel like quitting, we can keep going and growing *if we minister the way God tells us to in His Word.*

When I began my ministry back in 1950, I'm afraid I didn't have a clear vision of what Christian work was all about. Consequently, I floundered and was frustrated, not knowing exactly what to do or how to evaluate what I was doing. A Roman proverb says, "When the pilot does not know what port he is heading for, no wind is the right wind." I was certainly a bewildered pilot! Because I had received excellent training, I didn't lack for methods or ideas; but I wasn't clear as to *principles*. I was on the ocean of life with a road map instead of a compass, and I wasn't sure how to handle the rudder of the ship.

Now, many years and tears later, I think I have a limited grasp of a few of the principles of ministry; and I want to share them with you. As the familiar couplet puts it,

> Methods are many, principles are few;
> Methods always change, principles never do.

Certainly we need methods to serve God, but we must remember that methods work because of the principles behind them. To adopt a new method just because it worked for somebody else, without first understanding the principles behind that method, is to abandon both the compass and the rudder and start drifting helplessly on the tempestuous sea of service.

If you're frantically searching for guaranteed quick-fix methods, this book isn't for you because ministry is built on *basic principles*, not clever methods. God doesn't want us to have "ministry by imitation." He wants "ministry by incarnation," what Paul wrote about in Philippians 2:13: "For it is God who works in you both to will and to do for His good pleasure."

Let's begin with a definition of ministry that I've been using for several years. All definitions have their limitations, and this one isn't perfect; but it will at least keep us on the right track as we think together.

Ministry takes place when divine resources meet human needs through loving channels to the glory of God.

The kind of ministry this definition is talking about is best illustrated by an event recorded in Acts 3:

> Now Peter and John went up together to the temple at the hour of prayer, the ninth hour. And a certain man lame from his mother's womb was carried, whom they laid daily at the gate of the temple which is called Beautiful, to ask alms from those who entered the temple; who, seeing Peter and John about to go into the temple, asked for alms. And fixing his eyes on him, with John, Peter said, "Look at us." So he gave them his attention, expecting to receive something from them. Then Peter said, "Silver and gold I do not have, but what I do have I give you: In the name of Jesus Christ of Nazareth, rise up and walk." And he took him by the right hand and lifted him up, and immediately his feet and ankle bones received strength. So he, leaping up, stood and walked and entered the temple with them—walking, leaping, and praising God. And all the people saw him walking and praising God (vv. 1–9).

Here you have the four basic elements of ministry. Peter and John saw a man in great need: he was physically lame and spiritually dead. Manifesting the compassion of Christ, they shared God's power with him; and he was completely healed and soundly converted to Christ. God was glorified, opportunity was given to preach the gospel, and two thousand more people trusted Christ (Acts 2:41; 4:4).

So, if you and I are going to serve Jesus Christ—the way

God wants us to minister and the way the apostles ministered—we must (1) know the divine resources personally, (2) see the human needs compassionately, and (3) become channels of God's mighty resources so that (4) God alone is glorified. When God is glorified, His Spirit can work to bring Christ to those who need to know Him. In reaching one individual, Peter was able to reach the masses.

Before you turn to the next chapter, ponder this definition of ministry and examine your own heart. Do you know God personally and the marvelous resources that are available through Jesus Christ? Are you concerned about the needs of others so that you see them and want to help? Do you have compassion for those with needs? Are you willing to be a channel for God's glory?

Ministry takes place when divine resources meet human needs through loving channels to the glory of God.

I suggest you memorize this definition.

The trouble with too many of us is that we think God called us to be *manufacturers* when He really called us to be *distributors*. He alone has the resources to meet human needs; all we can do is receive His riches and share them with others. "Silver and gold I do not have," Peter announced, "but what I do have I give you" (Acts 3:6). When it comes to ministry, all of us are bankrupt, and only God is rich. Like Paul, we are "as poor, yet making many rich" (2 Cor. 6:10).

The miracle of Christ's feeding the five thousand comes to mind, the only miracle of Christ that is recorded in all four Gospels (Matt. 14:15–21; Mark 6:35–44; Luke 9:12–17; John 6:1–14). When the disciples saw more than five thousand hungry people before them, they didn't know what to do; but they made their suggestions just the same. As yet, they didn't really know how poor they were!

First, they advised Jesus to avoid the problem by sending

the crowd home. *Where was their compassion?* The Lord knew that the people were hungry and could never make the journey, so He rejected that plan. By the way, we are often tempted in ministry to get rid of the very people God wants us to help. The disciples did it more than once (Matt. 15:21–28; 19:13–15).

Philip admitted that there wasn't enough money on hand to buy food to feed such a big crowd, so a bigger budget wasn't the answer. (Most people think that having more money to spend is the solution to every problem.) Then Andrew found a boy with a small lunch of five barley loaves and two fish, a food supply totally inadequate to meet the need. "But what are they among so many?" Andrew asked (John 6:9), and the answer is, "Of themselves, they are nothing."

The disciples were trying to be manufacturers. They thought that it was *their* responsibility to come up with the money or the food or some clever way to solve the problem. But all the while, "He Himself knew what He would do" (John 6:6). *Jesus needed His disciples, not as manufacturers but as distributors.* He took the lad's lunch, looked up to heaven, blessed the food, broke it, and put it into the disciples' hands for them to feed the hungry multitude. The *multiplication* took place in His hands; the *distribution* was the work of the disciples' hands.

Once you accept yourself as a distributor of God's riches and not a manufacturer, you will experience a wonderful new freedom and joy in service. You won't be afraid of new challenges because you know God has the resources to meet them. You won't be frustrated trying to manufacture everything needed to get the job done; and when God blesses your work, you won't be tempted to take the credit. Dr. Bob Cook used to remind us in our Youth for Christ ministry, "If you can explain what's going on, God didn't do it!" That sounds like the experience of the Jews recorded in Psalm 126: "We were like those who dream. . . . The LORD has done great things for us, and we are glad" (vv. 1, 3). *How do you explain a miracle?* You don't! You just receive it and share it and let God have all the glory.

What are the divine resources that God makes available to His servants for their ministry? The word that best summarizes it is the familiar word *grace*: "And of His fullness we have all received, and grace for grace" (John 1:16). The image here seems to be that of an ocean, with wave after wave coming in to shore in unending fullness. I'm reminded of the poor woman who had her first view of the ocean and stood on the shore weeping. When asked why she was weeping, she replied, "It's so good to see something that there's plenty of!"

You don't *earn* grace, and you don't *deserve* grace; you simply receive it as God's loving gift and then share it with others. In ministry, we are *channels* of God's resources, not *reservoirs*: "Give, and it will be given to you: good measure, pressed down, shaken together, and running over will be put into your bosom. For with the same measure that you use, it will be measured back to you" (Luke 6:38). It's a basic law of the kingdom of God that the servants who know how poor they are become the richest, and those who give the most receive the most and therefore have the most to give.

Because we have a "manufacturer mentality," we're prone to depend on our own resources, things like experience, training, money, talent, and education. God can sanctify and use these assets, but they become liabilities apart from the grace of God. With all of his abilities and training, the apostle Paul knew that the secret of his effective ministry was the grace of God. "But by the grace of God I am what I am," he wrote to the Corinthians. "I labored more abundantly than they all, yet not I, but the grace of God which was with me" (1 Cor. 15:10). By God's grace, Paul was what he was, and Paul did what he did.

As God's children and God's servants, we can draw upon the riches of His grace (Eph. 1:7; 2:7), the riches of His glory (Eph. 3:16; Phil. 4:19), unsearchable riches (Eph. 3:8), the riches of His mercy (Eph. 2:4), the riches of His wisdom (Rom. 11:33), and much more: "And God is able to make all grace abound toward you, that you, always having all sufficiency in all things, may have an abundance for every good work" (2 Cor. 9:8).

So, one of the first steps we must take before our service can be used of God is to *confess our bankruptcy and receive by faith the grace that we need for acceptable service.* Just as we were saved by grace, through faith (Eph. 2:8–9), so we must work by grace, through faith, as we seek to minister. Only then can God work in and through us for His glory.

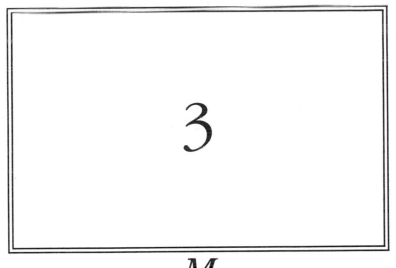

3

*M*inistry takes place when divine resources *meet human needs*.

In ministry, we're called to live for others. Ministry is not just another way of making a living; it's a wonderful opportunity for making a life, a life that's lived for others. It's an opportunity to be like the Lord Jesus Christ. When He was here on earth, He met human needs, all kinds of needs; and He wasn't always thanked or even appreciated. In fact, one man He healed turned state's evidence and got Jesus into trouble with the authorities (John 5:1–16).

We live in a world filled with people who have incredible needs of all kinds, and we can relate to these needs in one of several ways. We can *be blind to them and live our own lives*, but then we wouldn't be living as Christians are supposed to live. We certainly wouldn't be living like the Lord Jesus: "Let nothing be done through selfish ambition or conceit, but in lowliness of mind let each esteem others better [more important] than himself. Let each of you look out not only for his own interests, but also for the interests of others" (Phil. 2:3–4).

Or we can *take advantage of those needs to benefit ourselves.* Yes, it's possible to be in ministry and *use* people to get what we want instead of helping people to get what they need. The Pharisees, for example, used the common people to build their own authority instead of using their authority to build the people (Matt. 23:1–12). If we aren't careful, we can minister in such a way that we exploit the needs of others to get ourselves recognition, position, titles, honors, and privileges. *True servants of God help others whether they themselves get anything out of it or not.* Their concern is only that God be glorified and people trust Christ.

A third way we can relate to the needs of others is *to know about them but do nothing.* That is what the priest and the Levite did when they saw that battered Jew dying by the side of the Jericho road (Luke 10:25–37). Both saw the needy man and "passed by on the other side" instead of stopping to show mercy. Granted, it's impossible for us as God's servants to do something about *every* need that we see or hear about; but we must never be thankful for a reason (or an excuse) to escape responsibility, and we must guard against the kind of professionalism that leads to a hard heart.

In Christian service, a sensitive spirit and a tender heart are absolutely essential; but we can easily become calloused. Then our work becomes routine and perfunctory, and we say with the backslidden priests of Malachi's day, "Oh, what a weariness!" (Mal. 1:13). The Scottish minister and novelist George Macdonald, whose books so influenced C. S. Lewis, wrote, "Nothing is so deadening to the divine as an habitual dealing with the outsides of holy things." That's the best definition of religious professionalism I've ever read.

No, we must have neither a blind eye nor an averted eye, nor should we think only of ourselves when we see the needs of others. The only right way for the servant of God to respond is to ask, "Lord, what do You want me to do?" (Acts 9:6). We can't do everything, but we can do something; and we must do it as Jesus would so that He might be glorified.

The people God calls us to serve have all kinds of needs—physical, emotional, relational, financial—but at rock bottom their greatest need is *to be rightly related to God and His will.* That doesn't mean the Word of God and prayer will pay their bills or feed their stomachs. We don't quote a Bible promise to hungry people, pray for them, smile, and say, "Depart in peace, be warmed and filled" (James 2:16). We do what we can to put food on the table. But unless we help people grow into a right relationship with God, whatever help we give will be only a stopgap measure, a quick fix until the next time they have a need; and then the cycle is repeated.

Perhaps that is one of the major differences between Christian ministry and mere humanitarian benevolence, as helpful as it may be. Both can be done in love; both can put food on the table and shoes on the feet; but only true Christian ministry can put grace in the heart so that lives are changed and problems are really solved. The best thing we can do for people is not to solve their problems for them but so relate them to God's grace that they will be enabled to solve their problems and not repeat them.

It has been said that "the heart of every problem is the problem in the heart"; but the statement is only partly true. Sometimes it isn't what *we* have done that creates the difficulty but what *others* have done. Children sometimes suffer from what their parents do, and the opposite is also true. The company president embezzles money and wrecks the business, and scores of innocent workers are out of jobs. People may not cause their own problems, but if they relate to their problems the wrong way, they will make the problems worse. What life does to us depends on what life finds in us, and that is where the grace of God comes in.

The church is the body of Christ on earth, taking the place of the Savior who has returned to heaven. He "did not come to be served, but to serve, and to give His life a ransom for many" (Matt. 20:28); and that must be our attitude: sacrifice and service to the glory of God.

There was a time when Peter didn't say, "What I do have I give you" (Acts 3:6). He said, "See, we have left all and followed You. Therefore what shall we have?" (Matt. 19:27). Selfishness says, "What will I get?" Service says, "What I have I'll give to you."

The human needs in our world today are indescribable, innumerable, and (if you have a tender heart) almost unbearable. You and I can't do everything, but we can do something; and that something is the ministry God has called us to fulfill.

4

I ran across a new word in my reading: *Erinaceus*. It's a zoological term that describes the hedgehog family. Like hedgehogs, some people are as the genus Erinaceus: the closer you get to them, the more they stick you with their protective quills. You want to help them, but if you do, you're going to get hurt.

That's why we need *love*. Ministry takes place when divine resources meet human needs *through loving channels* to the glory of God. If the motivation for our service is anything less than Christ's love—His love for us and our love for Him—our ministry will not really meet human needs or glorify God: "But when He saw the multitudes, He was moved with compassion for them" (Matt. 9:36); "For the love of Christ compels us" (2 Cor. 5:14).

When I use the phrase "loving channels," I don't mean to imply that God's servants are passive conduits through whom God pours His blessing, come what may. God works not *in spite of* us or *instead of* us ("Let go and let God!") but *in* us and *through* us. And as He's working to share His divine resources with others, He wants to bless the channel as well. *If the worker doesn't get a blessing out of the work, something is radically wrong.* Serving God isn't punishment; it's nourishment. Jesus said, "My food is to do the will of Him who sent Me, and to finish His work" (John 4:34).

Serving God means working with people; and people not only *have* problems, but they can *be* problems because of the way they deal with their own needs. They can grow invisible protective quills to keep others at a distance; and unless you really love these people, you can never help them.

We learned in the previous chapter that you and I must rightly relate to the needs of others. We must not be blind to their needs or ignore them, nor must we use their needs as opportunities to promote ourselves. *But the people we're trying to help may take any or all of these same approaches to their own problems!* Some people are blind to their real needs and constantly want to go on a detour. Other people choose to ignore their needs and perhaps blame somebody else. And there are people who have learned to "exploit" their needs to get what they want from others. They can't afford to solve their problems because their whole life-style is built on them. This third group is perhaps the hardest to help.

We must remember, nevertheless, that we are loving channels of the *grace of God*. As Bernard of Clairvaux said, "Justice seeks out the merits of the case, but pity only regards the need." We who are servants of God don't deserve His grace any more than the ones we are serving deserve it, and who are we to limit God's grace and mercy?

However, Christian love is not blind. Paul prayed for the believers in Philippi that their love might "abound still more and more in knowledge and all discernment" (Phil 1:9). Jesus loved the young man we call the rich young ruler (Mark 10:21), but that didn't motivate Him to lower the standards and make it easy for the man to follow Christ. It isn't enough for us merely to love suffering people and want to help them. We must also love the truth that God has given us (Ps. 119:97; 2 Thess. 2:10). If truth and love contradict each other, something is amiss.

Many of us confess that we're not capable of loving people the way Jesus loves them and us. We do our best to practice 1 Corinthians 13, but it doesn't always last. But that's the "manufacturer mentality" again. God doesn't ask us to *work up* our Christian love in our own strength because He offers to create it within us when we need it: "The love of God has been poured out in our hearts by the Holy Spirit who was given to us" (Rom. 5:5); "But the fruit of the Spirit is love" (Gal. 5:22).

The love that we need for ministry is not a natural ability; it's a supernatural quality that only God can provide. When the people we serve irritate us or disappoint us, the first thing we usually do is pray for them and tell the Lord to change them. What we ought to do first is *pray for ourselves and ask God to increase our love.* Otherwise, we may give the devil a foothold in our own hearts, which will create problems the next time we try to minister to those people: "And be kind to one another [even if they aren't kind to you], tenderhearted [even if they hurt you], forgiving one another, even as God in Christ forgave you" (Eph. 4:32).

I'll have more to say later about the work of the Holy Spirit in ministry, but this much needs to be said now: the Holy Spirit can make you adequate for any ministry challenge God brings to you. In fact, God often allows problem people to come into your life so that you'll learn to depend more on His power and not your own resources.

Now is a good time to point out a truth about Christian service that for some reason we overlook: *God is as concerned about the servant as He is the service.* If all God wanted to do was get the work done, He could send His angels, and they would do it better and faster. But He not only wants to do something *through* us, He also wants to do something *in* us; and that is why the "hedgehogs" show up in our lives. God uses them to encourage us to pray, trust the Word, and depend on the Spirit for love and grace. Difficult people and difficult circumstances can be used by the Spirit to help us grow and become more like Christ.

However, when these difficulties come, our tendency is to pray for deliverance instead of growth. We ask the Lord, *"How* can I get out of this?" instead of *"What* can I get out of this?" When we do that, we miss the opportunities God gives us to develop spiritual maturity.

Sometimes you feel like quitting and running away, and that's the worst thing you can do. Resigning from your church, giving up your Sunday school class, leaving the committee, or abandoning the choir will never solve the problems or meet the needs in your heart. You'll probably meet the same situation and the same people (with different names) in the next ministry you accept. Why? Because God won't let His servants run away. God is determined that His children be "conformed to the image of His Son" (Rom. 8:29), and He will keep working until He accomplishes His purpose.

It's human to want to run away from a tough situation. Many believers have done it, and many more have wanted to do it. Moses had such a difficult time with Israel that he wanted to die (Num. 11:10–15), and Elijah became so discouraged that he deserted his post and went into the wilderness where he asked to die (1 Kings 19). Dr. V. Raymond Edman used to tell the Wheaton (Illinois) College students, "It's always too soon to quit." On the flyleaf of my copy of his book *The Disciplines of Life*, Dr. Edman wrote, "Remember always to keep chin up and knees down!" Good counsel!

You'll meet problem people and problem situations wherever you go, so make up your mind to expect them, accept them, and let God use them in your life. The devil wants to use problem people as weapons to tear you down, but the Spirit can use them as tools to build you up. The choice is yours. If you stay on the job and trust God to work, you'll experience His grace in a wonderful way; and you'll be a better servant. *One of the best ways to discover the divine resources that others need is to need them yourself and trust God to supply them.* Paul wrote,

Blessed be the God and Father of our Lord Jesus Christ, the Father of mercies and God of all comfort, who comforts us in all our tribulation, that we may be able to comfort those who are in any trouble, with the comfort with which we ourselves are comforted by God (2 Cor. 1:3–4).

Martin Luther said that prayer, meditation, and temptation make a minister, and he was right. Jesus was "in all points tempted as we are" (Heb. 4:15) that He might be able to understand our needs and adequately meet them, and we sometimes suffer for the same reason. The prophet Ezekiel wrote, "Then I came to the captives at Tel Abib, who dwelt by the River Chebar; and I sat where they sat" (Ezek. 3:15). *I sat where they sat.* That's the posture of the true servant of Jesus Christ who wants to be a loving channel of the grace of God.

In Christian ministry, problems with people are among the

most difficult to bear; and the people who have—and cause—the greatest problems are those who need us the most. That's why we must be *loving* channels, no matter how people may respond to our ministry. It may take years before they allow the Lord to change them, and you may not even be on the scene when it happens. No matter; the Lord is at work, and He will finish what He has begun (Phil. 1:6).

5

We've considered briefly three of the four elements involved in Christian ministry: the divine resources, the human need, and the loving channels. The fourth element, the glory of God, is the most important because the glory of God is what salvation and ministry are all about. He saved us "to the praise of the glory of His grace" (Eph. 1:6, 12, 14), and He commands us, "Whatever you do, do all to the glory of God" (1 Cor. 10:31).

If our motive for serving is anything other than the glory of God, what we do will be only religious activity and not true Christian ministry. We may help people in one way or another, but God will not be able to bless as He wants to do. If undetected, a counterfeit bill can do a lot of good as it passes from hand to hand; but when it gets to the bank—the final place of judgment—it will be rejected: "Therefore judge nothing before the time, until the Lord comes, who will both bring to light the hidden things of darkness and reveal the counsels [motives] of the hearts. Then each one's praise will come from God" (1 Cor. 4:5).

The phrase "the glory of God" is difficult to pin down. How do we know when what we're doing is really glorifying God? For one thing, we can't explain what's happening, and often nobody expected it to happen. Remember my quotation from Bob Cook? "If you can explain what's going on, God didn't do it!"

When evangelist D. L. Moody was preaching in Birmingham, England, in 1875, the noted Congregational theologian and preacher Dr. R. W. Dale cooperated in the campaign. After listening to Moody preach and seeing the blessings, Dr. Dale wrote in his denomination's magazine: "I told Mr. Moody that the work was most plainly of God, for I could see no real relation between him and what he had done. He laughed cheerily, and said he should be very sorry if it were otherwise."[1]

The working of God isn't always predictable. Because the wind of the Spirit "blows where it wishes" (John 3:8), we have to be alert to set our sails in the right direction. It's possible to "succeed" in Christian work and be a failure in Christian ministry. "In whatever man does without God," wrote George Macdonald, "he must fail miserably—or succeed more miserably." A sobering thought! The psalmist declared, "And He gave them their request, but sent leanness into their soul" (Ps. 106:15).

God is glorified when people see the Lord and not the servant: "Let your light so shine before men, that they may see your good works and glorify your Father in heaven" (Matt. 5:16). You have to decide whether you will be a servant or a celebrity, whether you will magnify Christ or promote yourself (Phil. 1:20–21). Because we don't always understand our own motives, it's possible to be in Christian service for reasons other than the glory of the Lord. Some people are involved in ministry only for personal gain. Perhaps they relish the authority and recognition that are often associated with ministry, or maybe they just enjoy having opportunities to display their talents. It's doubtful that anybody ever does anything out of a purely unselfish motive; but with God's help, we can try.

God is glorified when people see the Master and not the minister. The moderator of a Presbyterian church in Melbourne, Australia, gave J. Hudson Taylor a flattering introduction. When the founder of the China Inland Mission stepped into the pulpit, he quietly said, "Dear friends, I am the little servant of an illustrious Master." The late A. W. Tozer was once presented to a congregation in a similar manner, and his response was, "All I can say is, dear God, forgive him for what he said—and forgive me for enjoying it so much!"[2]

God is jealous of His glory: "I am the LORD, that is My name; and My glory I will not give to another" (Isa. 42:8). In Isaiah's day, the problem was idols, worshiping the false gods of the enemy, a problem that is still with us today. When a political candidate appears on television, the most important member of his team is not the speech writer but the image maker, the media expert who "sells" the candidate to the viewers. When you find yourself more concerned about your "image" than your character and your work, you have stopped glorifying God.

When your service produces fruit, God is glorified. "By this My Father is glorified," said Jesus, "that you bear much fruit" (John 15:8). There is a difference between "fruit" and "results." You can get "results" by following surefire formulas, manipulating people, or turning on your charisma; but "fruit" comes from life. When the Spirit of life is working through the Word of life, the seed planted bears fruit; *and that fruit has in it the seed for more fruit* (Gen. 1:11–12).

Results are counted and soon become silent statistics, but living fruit remains and continues to multiply to the glory of God (John 15:16).

Let me suggest one more evidence that your work is glorifying God: the enemy opposes what you're doing. Paul announced, "For a great and effective door has opened to me, and there are many adversaries" (1 Cor. 16:9). Opportunities and adversaries usually go together, and adversaries can create new opportunities. Satan encourages those who magnify themselves and depend on the flesh, but he hates it when the Spirit of God is at work bringing glory to Jesus Christ.

Problems in ministry will present two opportunities to you: the opportunity to glorify God, or the opportunity to glorify yourself. The experience of Moses, recorded in Exodus 32, illustrates this truth. While Moses was on the mount, getting his instructions from the Lord, the people of Israel became impatient and asked Aaron to make them a new god. Aaron made a golden calf, and the people held a feast that involved not only idolatry but immorality.

Of course, the Lord knew what was going on, and He informed Moses: "Your people whom you brought out of the land of Egypt have corrupted themselves" (v. 7). Then God tested Moses by making him an offer: He would destroy Israel and create a new and greater nation of Moses and his descendants (v. 10). A lesser man would have jumped at the chance to be the founder of a new nation, but Moses turned it down. Instead, he pleaded with the Lord to forgive His people because *Moses' great concern was the glory of the Lord.* In fact, Moses was willing to lay down his own life so that Israel might be spared (vv. 30–35).

The people of Israel didn't know the battles Moses was fighting for them on the mount, just as your people don't know the struggles that you go through on their behalf. But personal sacrifice is an insignificant thing when you live and serve for the glory of God alone.

I trust that one day, you and I will be able to say to the Father what Jesus said to Him: "I have glorified You on the earth. I have finished the work which You have given Me to do" (John 17:4).

Remember always to heed these words: "Therefore, whether you eat or drink, or whatever you do, do all to the glory of God" (1 Cor. 10:31).

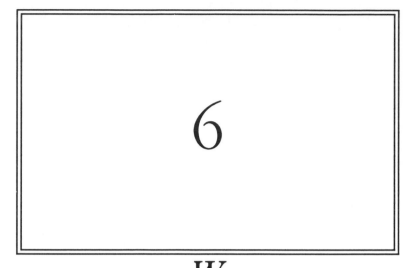

6

We've covered the basics of ministry given in my suggested definition, but much more needs to be said. Now we need to apply these principles to various aspects of Christian service so that you can put them to work in your life.

I've been emphasizing the fact that ministry is not something we do for God but something God does in and through us: "For it is God who works in you both to will and to do for His good pleasure" (Phil. 2:13). The "willing" and the "working" both come from God. Whatever God calls us to do, we *can* do with His help; otherwise, He would never have called us: "He who calls you is faithful, who also will do it" (1 Thess. 5:24).

When God called Moses to ministry (Exod. 3–4), Moses resisted the call because he didn't feel he could do what God wanted him to do. He asked, "Who am I that I should go to Pharaoh, and that I should bring the children of Israel out of Egypt?" (Exod. 3:11). Moses argued that he was "slow of speech and slow of tongue" (Exod. 4:10), and God reminded Moses that He had made his tongue and could easily teach him what to say.

Such resistance isn't unusual. After all, it's an awesome thing to be God's servant and do His will. Like marriage, Christian service should not be "entered into lightly or carelessly, but reverently, soberly and in the fear of God," as *The Book of Common Prayer* puts it. But it's one thing to *resist* the call of God and quite another thing to *refuse* it. That's what Jonah did, and God kept after him until he said a reluctant yes. But what a price Jonah paid!

If God has called you to minister, no matter what that ministry may be, *He hasn't made a mistake.* He knows what He's doing, and the best thing you can do is gratefully submit to His will and trust Him to work.

God always prepares His servants before He calls them, and this preparation begins long before birth. Your very genetic structure is ordained of God! "Before I formed you in the womb I knew you," God told frightened young Jeremiah. "Before you were born I sanctified you; I ordained you a prophet to the nations" (Jer. 1:5). And this is what David had to say:

> For You formed my inward parts;
> You covered [wove] me in my mother's womb.
> I will praise You, for I am
>   fearfully and wonderfully made. . . .
> My frame was not hidden from You,
> When I was made in secret. . . .
> Your eyes saw my substance,
>   being yet unformed.
> And in Your book they all were written,
> The days fashioned for me,
> When as yet there were none of them (Ps. 139:13–16).

During my childhood, I was frustrated because I didn't have the abilities other boys had, especially in athletics and the manual arts. I was the last one chosen for every team, and I passed my junior high school shop courses mainly because the instructors liked my two older brothers, both of whom are good craftsmen. Believe me, those school years weren't easy; and there were times when I was bitter. "Why me, God?"

But God didn't prepare me to be an athlete, a woodworker, or a mechanic. He wanted me to be a preacher and a writer, and He arranged for that when He planned my genetic structure. He did the same thing for you, and He knew what He was doing. Instead of complaining about what we don't have, let's thank God for what we do have *and find out why He gave it to us.* Your abilities and interests are an important part of the will of God for your life.

This point leads to a second consideration: in your ministry, you must be yourself. One of the tragedies in the church today is that too many people are trying to imitate "the greats" instead of ministering the way God wants them to minister. You are unique in what you are and what you can do, and God doesn't want you to destroy that uniqueness by your trying to be somebody else. To be sure,we can learn from one another, and there's nothing wrong with appreciating God's special servants and being inspired and instructed by them. But God forbid that we should imitate them and destroy our own distinctive ministry! Be yourself—your *best* self—and God will use you in a special way.

Here's a third suggestion: build on your strengths, and ask God for helpers who can compensate for your weaknesses. Nobody's perfect, and nobody can do everything. There are gifted musicians who can train choirs and present splendid concerts, but they have problems preparing and following budgets. I have preacher friends who are masters of the pulpit but miserable in the counseling room. Not all preachers are good administrators, and some excellent missionaries are not gifted pulpiteers. It's no disgrace to admit your limitations and seek help in strengthening them: "For I say, through the grace given to me, to everyone who is among you, not to think of himself more highly than he ought to think, but to think soberly, as God has dealt to each one a measure of faith" (Rom. 12:3).

We were all born with different interests and abilities, and when we were saved, we were given different gifts. I believe God matches spiritual gifts with natural abilities so that we can fill the place He has for us and do the job He wants us to do. Paul makes this clear: "But now God has set the members, each one of them, in the body just as He pleased. And if they were all one member, where would the body be?" (1 Cor. 12:18–19).

There's something in human nature that makes us want to have what the other person has. The evangelist wants to be a theologian, the singer wants to preach, and the preacher wants to sing! Granted, some five-talent people can do many things, and there's nothing wrong with a godly ambition to do more; but most of us have to settle for being faithful with the one or two talents God's given us. If we're faithful, we'll get the same reward as the five-talent people who are faithful. It's not how much we have to start with that really counts but what we have to show for it at the end.

7

Those of us who minister must put others ahead of ourselves, but we must put the Lord ahead of others. "Ourselves your bondservants for Jesus' sake" (2 Cor. 4:5) gives you the right order of priority. Of the three persons involved in ministry—the Lord, the minister, and the person ministered to—the Lord must come first.

I've counted at least eleven places in the Law of Moses where he tells the priests that they "minister to the Lord" (see especially Exod. 28:1, 3, 4, 41). Certainly the priests were ministering to the people as they offered the sacrifices, taught the Word, and helped to settle their disputes; but the first responsibility of the priests was to the Lord and not to the people.

We find the same emphasis in the New Testament. It was while Barnabas and Saul were ministering to the Lord in the church at Antioch that the Spirit called them to missionary service (Acts 13:2). We have these words to guide us: "And whatever you do, do it heartily, as to the Lord and not to men, knowing that from the Lord you will receive the reward of the inheritance; for you serve the Lord Christ" (Col. 3:23–24). The order is Christ first, others second, ourselves last.

Focusing on serving the Lord can make a big difference in your ministry. For one thing, *you will be motivated to do your work and not look for excuses.* If you serve only to earn a salary, you will never do your best as long as you think you're underpaid. If you minister to get recognition, you will start doing less when people don't show their appreciation. The only motivation that will take you through the storms and keep you on the job is, "I'm serving Jesus Christ." Paul called himself "the bondslave of Jesus Christ," and slaves didn't have the privilege of saying no.

Another result of serving Christ first is that *you want to do your best.* The careless priests in Malachi's day weren't giving God their best, and He rebuked them for it. They were offering animals that were imperfect, "the blind . . . the stolen, the lame, and the sick" (Mal. 1:8, 13). "Offer it then to your governor!" the Lord reproached them. "Would he be pleased with you? Would he accept you favorably?" (Mal. 1:8).

Most of us confess that when we do something for somebody we really love, somebody who means a great deal to us, we work hard to give our best. No demand is too difficult, and no sacrifice is too great. When Jacob labored seven years to get Rachel for his wife, those seven years of toil "seemed only a few days to him because of the love he had for her" (Gen. 29:20).

"I never made a sacrifice," said missionary David Livingstone. "We ought not to talk of 'sacrifice' when we remember the great sacrifice which He made who left His Father's throne on high to give Himself for us."[1] At the age of fifty-two, C. T. Studd left everything to go to Africa, and people told him he was foolish. Studd's reply was, "If Jesus Christ be God and died for me, then no sacrifice can be too great for me to make for Him."[2]

When you put Christ first in your ministry and do your work "as to the Lord," you not only do more and do your best, but *the burden is light*. Contrary to what the man said in the parable of the talents, Jesus Christ is not "a hard man" for whom it is difficult to work (Matt. 25:14–30). "For My yoke is easy and My burden is light" is His promise (Matt. 11:30); and it's true.

I would rather have Jesus Christ as my Master than anyone else I know. He loves me, He knows all about me, He made me, He knows the future, and He gives me the power I need to serve Him acceptably and fruitfully. When I fail, He forgives me and helps me start over again. He never leaves me or forsakes me, and He rewards me graciously, though I don't deserve it. Could you want a better Master than that?

Something else happens when you put Jesus Christ first in your ministry: *you stop watching other Christians and passing judgment on what they do or what God does with them.* People watching is a popular pastime among Christian workers, but it's a dangerous one. If you keep your eyes of faith on Christ and seek to please Him alone, you won't have either the time or the desire to watch others.

Read again the parable of the workers in the vineyard (Matt. 20:1–16), a story Jesus told in response to Peter's question, "What shall we have?" (Matt. 19:27). The first workers that were hired made two mistakes: they demanded a guaranteed wage, and when they got what they asked for, they complained about it. Why? Because they were watching the other workers to see how long they had worked and how much they were paid. "These last men have worked only one hour," they complained, "and you made them equal to us who have borne the burden and the heat of the day" (Matt. 20:12).

Have you ever complained because God gave others a better deal than He gave you? Perhaps the people don't seem to work as hard as you do, or maybe they haven't been in Christian service as long as you have; yet God bypassed you and rewarded them abundantly. Satan can use a thing like that to get a foothold in your life, make you bitter, and create problems in your ministry.

But if you're working for Christ alone, you won't be bothered by what other workers do or what God does for them. Nor will you try to make bargains with God to be sure you get your rightful share. If you do, you'll be the loser because God still gives His best to those who let Him write the contract.

Some years ago, I found myself fretting like those workers in the parable, complaining to God about the way He was mistreating me and blessing another worker I'd been watching. At Sunday morning worship, our pastor was away, and the guest speaker was Dr. Vernon Grounds, then president of the Conservative Baptist Seminary in Denver. When he read his text, I knew I was undone: "What is that to thee? follow thou me" (John 21:22 KJV). As he expounded the text, Dr. Grounds quoted it frequently; and each time he quoted his text, the Word stabbed my heart. I had to have a private meeting with God right there in the pew and confess that, like Peter, I had gotten my eyes off Christ and was looking at others. In later years, when I've been tempted to complain, the text has come back to me and helped me turn my eyes on Jesus.

Ministry isn't easy, but you make it more difficult for yourself if you serve *people* instead of the Lord Jesus

Christ. You can't please everybody, so don't even try. Just live and work in such a way that your Master will be able to say, "You are My beloved servant in whom I am well pleased."

8

I firmly believe that God has a specific plan for each of His children and that He wants to share his plan with us and help us fulfill it. At least that's the way I interpret Paul's words in Ephesians 2:10: "For we are His workmanship, created in Christ Jesus for good works, which God prepared beforehand that we should walk in them."

" 'For good works' is not a narrow phrase referring merely to specific acts of so-called Christian service," said G. Campbell Morgan in a sermon on this text. He explained that "it refers to the whole life. . . . He has foreordained the works of the man He is making. He has been ahead of me preparing the place to which I am coming, manipulating all the resources of the universe in order that the work I do may be a part of His whole great and gracious work."[1]

Since God made me the way I am, and Psalm 139 seems to teach that, He must have a purpose in view. Everything in the universe accomplishes some divine purpose; and it seems unreasonable that we who are made in the image of God, and redeemed by the sacrifice of His Son, should be left out. John of Damascus defined *providence* as "the care God takes of all existing things." If not one sparrow is forgotten before God (Luke 12:6), surely the Father cares for and guides His own children!

Paul's words to the Ephesians don't teach fatalism. Obedience to the will of God gives you wings, not chains! You are never more free than when you fulfill the plan God has for your life. This plan is not an impersonal machine that will break down when you disobey, leaving you with a wrecked life that can never be repaired. In Ephesians 2:10, God is pictured not as a mechanic but as a potter. If the clay refuses to yield, the potter doesn't give up: "And the vessel that he made of clay was marred in the hand of the potter; so he made it again into another vessel, as it seemed good to the potter to make" (Jer. 18:4).

Moses began his ministry by defending a fellow Jew and then fleeing for his life, but God made him again. When things got tough, Abraham ran off to Egypt, and twice he lied about his wife; but God made him again. Isaac lied about his wife, and Jacob schemed his way through life; but God made them again. And those men were the patriarchs who founded the Hebrew nation!

When we investigate the lives of the apostles, the record doesn't improve too much. We all know about Peter's failures, climaxing in his denying Christ three times. But what about James and John wanting to call fire from heaven to destroy a whole village? (Jesus nicknamed them "the sons of thunder"!) And don't forget the times the apostles argued among themselves over who was the greatest. Those things shouldn't have happened, but they did. However, the failures of those men didn't stop God from accomplishing His purposes because He made them again and used them in a mighty way.

Now, lest we should get overconfident and recklessly tempt God, we need to read Jeremiah 19 and see the prophet *breaking the vessel because it was beyond repair.* It's possible for God's servants to resist God so willfully that they cease to be vessels "for honor, sanctified and useful for the Master, prepared for every good work" (2 Tim. 2:21). That's what happened to Samson and King Saul, and God had to remove them from the scene. As the writer to the Hebrews said, "It is a fearful thing to fall into the hands of the living God" (Heb. 10:31).

If a servant of God falls, let's obey the command of Galatians 6:1 and seek to "restore such a one in a spirit of gentleness, considering [ourselves] lest [we] also be tempted." That restoration process may take years, but let's not give up. The purpose of discipline is restoration, and the results of restoration ought to be fellowship and ministry. The restored servant may not be able to go back to the original place of leadership, but surely the Spirit of God has some place of ministry in the vast harvest field where laborers are still desperately needed.

The God of creation and redemption is also the God of history who is at work in the affairs of nations. He sent Joseph to Egypt to get things ready for Jacob and his family so that He might build a mighty nation. He had Moses born at just the right time to deliver Israel from bondage. He prepared Joshua to lead the people victoriously into the promised land. He gave barren Hannah her long-prayed-for son and then used him to bring the wayward nation back to His covenant. *Those things were not accidents; they were appointments.* Every Bible biography bears witness to the truth of Ephesians 2:10.

But what does the truth of Ephesians 2:10 mean to you and me in our Christian service? It gives us confidence and courage when the enemy attacks us or when our work seems to be in vain. Joseph cast into a prison, David taken flight from King Saul, Jeremiah persecuted by a religious but godless nation, and Daniel thrown into a lions' den—all testify to the fact that *when God calls you, He enables you and He sees you through.* By nature, Jeremiah was a tender youth who would have preferred the routine work of a priest rather than the hazardous calling of a prophet; but God's calling gave him the confidence he needed. God said to him,

> For behold, I have made you this day
> A fortified city and an iron pillar,
> And bronze walls against the whole land (Jer. 1:18).

When my wife and I were serving in our first pastorate, God made it clear that the church had to build a new sanctuary. The idea frightened me for several reasons. For one thing, the economy was suffering in our area; and our membership was neither large nor wealthy. Some of the bank officials we talked to only smiled and advised us not to build. I'm not skilled at reading blueprints and would have a hard time building a birdhouse, let alone constructing a church edifice.

One morning, during my devotional time, one of my chapters for the day was 1 Chronicles 28, King David's instructions for building the temple. When I read verse 10, I almost jumped out of my chair:

Consider now, for the LORD has chosen you to build a house for the sanctuary; be strong, and do it.

And verse 20 just about put me into orbit:

And David said to his son Solomon, "Be strong and of good courage, and do it; do not fear nor be dismayed, for the LORD God—my God—will be with you. He will not leave you nor forsake you, until you have finished all the work for the service of the house of the LORD."

I don't know how many times I turned to these promises during the difficult months of that building program because they were my anchor in the storms and my light in the darkness. *God kept His promises—He always does—and helped us do what humanly speaking we were unable to do.*

Now, I'm not one of those superstitious persons who seeks God's direction by opening my Bible just anywhere and pointing to a verse. But when the Spirit of God impresses me with a passage *in the course of my regular Bible reading,* I stop and pay attention. I don't read my Bible in the past tense. Our God is the God of the living, who dwells in the eternal present; and I believe He wants to communicate with me each day through His Word. God not only has a special plan for my life, but He wants to reveal that plan to me and help me fulfill it.

If you're serving in the will of God, you're like Esther: "You have come to the kingdom for such a time as this" (Esther 4:14). What God starts, He finishes (Phil. 1:6). If you decide to quit, He will lovingly discipline you until you're willing to obey, just as He did with Jonah. If you persist in your rebellion, He may put you on the shelf and label you "disqualified" (1 Cor. 9:27). God will get His work done either with you or without you (Esther 4:14), but you are the loser if you quit.

You must depend on the eternal purposes of God and the unchanging promises of God if you're to keep going when the going is tough. Take my word for it, the going *will* be tough; but God's purposes and promises will not fail.

*O*n October 2, 1840, the young Presbyterian pastor Robert Murray M'Cheyne wrote this letter to his friend Daniel Edwards who was leaving for Germany to train for missionary service:

My dear friend:
I trust you will have a pleasant and profitable time in Germany. I know you will apply hard to German; but do not forget the culture of the inner man—I mean of the heart. How diligently the cavalry officer keeps his saber clean and sharp; every stain he rubs off with the greatest care. Remember you are God's sword—His instrument—I trust a chosen vessel unto Him to bear His name. In great measure, according to the purity and perfections of the instrument, will be the success. It is not great talents God blesses so much as great likeness to Jesus. A holy minister is an awful weapon in the hand of God.[1]

I recall standing in the vestry of St. Peter's Church in Dundee, Scotland, and holding M'Cheyne's Bible in my hands. It was a high and holy hour, believe me! During the early years of my Christian walk, reading Bonar's *Memoirs and Remains of Robert Murray M'Cheyne* made a lasting impression on me; and I have frequently turned to this Christian classic for inspiration and instruction. M'Cheyne's example of godly living gave great power to his unforgettable words: "A holy minister is an awful weapon in the hand of God."

Certainly God wants to use our talents. After all, He gave them to us. But along with the developing of our talents and spiritual gifts is the perfecting of our character. To use M'Cheyne's metaphor, we are God's weapons; and if the weapon is to be effective, it must be polished and sharp.

You may not think of yourself as a weapon, but the metaphor is quite biblical. In Isaiah 49:2, Messiah is compared to a sharp sword and a polished arrow; and Zechariah 9:13 compares Zion's army to bows and arrows and "the sword of a mighty man." Paul used the image in Romans 6:13 where he admonished believers to yield their bodies to God "as instruments of righteousness"; and the word translated "instruments" means "tools" or "weapons."

Christian service means invading a battleground, not a playground; and you and I are the weapons God uses to attack and defeat the enemy. When God used Moses' rod, He needed Moses' hand to lift it. When God used David's sling, He needed David's hand to swing it. When God builds a ministry, He needs somebody's surrendered body to get the job done. *You are important to the Lord, so keep your life pure:* "A holy minister [servant] is an awful weapon in the hand of God."

There's no substitute for Christian character. No matter

how much talent and training we may have, if we don't have character, we don't have anything. To quote M'Cheyne again, words he spoke in 1840: "But oh, study universal holiness of life! Your whole usefulness depends on this. Your . . . sermon lasts but an hour or two—your life preaches all the week."[2] He was speaking at an ordination service, but the admonition applies to any form of Christian service. A holy life is a useful life.

The media scandals of a few years ago gave us a painful reminder that there's a Grand Canyon of difference between *reputation* and *character*, and that popularity isn't always a guarantee of spirituality. It's possible to get a following but not necessarily promote God's work. You can fool many of the people some of the time, but eventually the truth comes out.[3]

Life is built on character, but character is built on decisions. The decisions you make, small and great, do to your life what the sculptor's chisel does to the block of marble. *You are shaping your life by your thoughts, attitudes, and actions and becoming either more or less like Jesus Christ.* The more you are like Christ, the more God can trust you with His blessing.

The person who cultivates integrity realizes that there can be no division between "secular and sacred" in the Christian life; everything must be done to the glory of God (1 Cor. 10:31). God reminded two of His greatest leaders, Moses (Exod. 3:5) and Joshua (Josh. 5:15), that the servant of the Lord is *always* standing on holy ground and had better behave accordingly. If nobody else is watching, God is; and He will be our judge.

Character isn't the same as personality, although character affects personality. Too many Christians think they can "get by" in spiritual ministry because they have charisma and can

41

attract and hold an audience. But it takes more than a winning personality to influence people for Christ; it takes godly character. It's been said that people are like trees: the shadow of the tree is *reputation*, the fruit of the tree is *personality*, but the roots of the tree are the most important part—*character.*

Somebody asked the wealthy banker J. P. Morgan what the best collateral was for a loan, and Morgan replied, "Character." What is true in the financial world is true in the spiritual world. God gives His best to those who most reflect the beauty of holiness: "For the eyes of the LORD run to and fro throughout the whole earth, to show Himself strong on behalf of those whose heart is loyal to Him" (2 Chron. 16:9).

The word *holiness* puzzles some people and frightens others. When I was a young Christian, I avoided "holiness people" because I thought they were a strange breed of extremists or cultists. Well, perhaps a few of them were; but that doesn't mean that *holiness* is a bad word: "But as He who called you is holy, you also be holy in all your conduct, because it is written, 'Be holy, for I am holy'" (1 Pet. 1:15–16; Lev. 11:44–45). Holiness is to the inner person what health is to the body. Holiness is wholeness, Christlikeness, the fruit of the Spirit being revealed in our lives (Gal. 5:22–23).

Some people have made the cultivation of holiness into a private religious hobby. They enjoy fellowshipping with other victorious Christians, but they never seem to channel their blessings into world evangelism and the building of the church. The late Dag Hammarskjold said that "the road to holiness necessarily passes through the world of action."[4] Jesus asked, "But why do you call Me 'Lord, Lord,' and not do the things which I say?" (Luke 6:46). God doesn't make us holy so that we can enjoy it. He makes us holy so that He can use us to do the work He wants us to do.

In other words, holiness is a very practical thing, at least the way Peter described it:

> But . . . giving all diligence, add to your faith virtue, to virtue knowledge, to knowledge self-control, to self-control perseverance, to perseverance godliness, to godliness brotherly kindness, and to brotherly kindness love. For if these things are yours and abound, you will be neither barren [idle, useless] nor unfruitful in the knowledge of our Lord Jesus Christ (2 Pet. 1:5–8).

The Pharisees had a brand of artificial righteousness that was shallow, brittle, and toxic; and Jesus condemned it: "For I say to you, that unless your righteousness exceeds the righteousness of the scribes and Pharisees, you will by no means enter the kingdom of heaven" (Matt. 5:20). Instead of helping people, the Pharisees only added to their burdens; and whatever the Pharisees touched became defiled (Matt. 23:4, 25–28). It was a righteousness of legalistic rules and human-created standards that never penetrated the heart and transformed the life. That's not the kind of holiness God wants us to experience.

When Paul urged Timothy to exercise himself to godliness (1 Tim. 4:7–8), the apostle used a metaphor familiar to the people of that day. Both the Greeks and the Romans were devoted to athletics and took the contests seriously. However, unlike most ticket holders and TV watchers today, the ancients saw athletics as enrichment and not merely as entertainment. They would be shocked at our professional organized sports world, the prizes awarded and the large salaries paid. To participate in the Greek games, you had to meet some stringent requirements; and if you broke any of the rules, even during training, you were disqualified (2 Tim. 2:5). It was not a contest for either fame or money, but for the glory of your city and nation.

Yet the key to becoming a winning athlete is the same today as it was in Timothy's day: consistent discipline exercised under competent supervision. Greek boys began working out at the local gymnasium early in life, learning how to wrestle, box, run, swim, and participate in competitive games. The Greek ideal was "a sound mind in a sound body," and every boy strived for that ideal for the glory of his community.

The point Paul was making to Timothy was simply this: as God's children, we must put into our Christian living the same kind of discipline that athletes put into sports. Athletes have to sacrifice and say no even to good things. They must be totally devoted to the goal of becoming winners. Every decision they make is tested by one thing: Will it help to make me a winner?

A young preacher attended a "deeper life conference" and shared his "victory experience" with the noted Scottish preacher Alexander Whyte of Edinburgh. Whyte listened patiently and then replied, "Ay, it's a sair fecht [sore fight] up to the very last!"[5]

A holy life isn't the automatic consequence of reading the right books, listening to the right tapes, or attending the right meetings. It's the result of a living, loving union with Jesus Christ and a life marked by godly discipline. It means setting the alarm clock so we can begin the day with God and pray and meditate on the Word. It means following Paul's example of consecration *and concentration* and saying with him, "One thing I do" (Phil. 3:12–14). Olympic winners pay a price, but they figure it's worth it. Do we?

10

*I*f you had asked the apostle Paul what his goal was in serving God, he would have said, "That we may present every man perfect [mature] in Christ Jesus" (Col. 1:28). If you had asked him to describe the work of the local church, he would have replied, "For the equipping of the saints for the work of ministry, for the edifying of the body of Christ, till we all come to the unity of the faith and of the knowledge of the Son of God, to a perfect [mature] man, to the measure of the stature of the fullness of Christ" (Eph. 4:12–13).

In spite of what some "success preachers" say, God's goal for our lives is not money but maturity, not happiness but holiness, not getting but giving. God is at work making people more like His Son, and that's what Christian service is all about. Your purpose in serving isn't to build the biggest church or Sunday school class, the greatest choir, or the most efficient band of ushers. Your purpose is to build people of Christian character whom God can bless and use to build others. You can use all kinds of gimmicks and techniques to gather a crowd or build an organization, but that's not the same as building His church.

The key idea is maturity. The individual Christian is born into the family of God and should mature and become more like Jesus Christ. As the church body matures, it increases in size and takes on adult features and adult responsibilities. It, too, becomes more like Christ. There's no conflict between size and maturity, although all bodies don't mature exactly alike. But where there's life, there ought to be growth.

There's nothing automatic about spiritual maturity. Paul had to pray for believers, share the Word with them, warn them, even discipline them, to bring them out of babyhood and into adulthood (1 Cor. 3:1–4). Paul wasn't always successful in helping people mature, nor will we be; but with the Lord's help, he did his best. If people failed to mature, the failure was theirs and not Paul's.

The danger is that we exploit people to get things done instead of ministering to them so that what they're doing helps them mature in Christ. Remember, in God's eyes, the worker is more important than the work. If the worker is what he or she ought to be, the work will be done right and will please God.

People minister in a maturing way when they know what to do, how to do it, why they're doing it, and how their work fits into the total plan of God for the church. (Of course, their motive must be to glorify God, but we've already discussed that.) Thrusting people into jobs without first giving them preparation is like throwing nonswimmers into the ocean without life jackets.

I recall the first time I read Scripture in public. I was a young Christian, and one of the church leaders thought it was time I did something in the church. Just before morning worship began, he told me he would call me to the platform to read Luke 3:1–6; and he rushed away to meet with the pastor. Words like *tetrarch, Iturea, Trachonitis, Lysanias,* and *Abilene* were foreign to me (do *you* know how to pronounce them correctly?), and I didn't own a self-pronouncing Bible. I'm sure I could have borrowed one, but I was too paralyzed to make a wise decision like that. My platform debut was a disaster, and I went home embarrassed.[1]

I had a similar experience some months later at a street meeting. I went along to help with the singing and to pass out tracts; but on the spot, I was publicly called on to give my testimony. There were a few teenagers in the small audience we'd gathered; and if I had been prepared, I could have said something useful to them. As it was, I stammered through my story and quoted the few Bible verses I'd learned in confirmation class. Again, I experienced a ministry disaster.

At this point, you may be saying, "Yes, but God can take what we think are disasters and use them in ways we won't know about until we get to heaven." I agree, and it's possible that my bungling brought somebody blessing; *but why tempt the Lord?* If He can bless disasters, just think of what blessing He could give if we're really prepared!

One of the greatest compliments God's servants can receive is this: "Being a part of your ministry is really helping me to grow." Remember, where there's real fruit, there's seed in it for more fruit. Ministry means that God uses us to create a spiritual atmosphere that encourages others to grow and become fruitful in the Lord. Christian educator Dr. Ted Ward says it best: "Leadership is a serving relationship that has the effect of facilitating human development."[2]

11

*W*hen our older daughter was a child in grade school, one day she came storming into the house, slammed the door, stomped into her room, slammed that door, all the while muttering under her breath, "People— *people!*—PEOPLE!"

Thinking I might be of some help, I tapped on the door and asked, "May I come in?"

The answer was an explosive "No!"

"Why?" I asked.

"Because you're a people!"

Even children have their problems with people. One thing's for sure: believers who try to serve the Lord can expect to have problems with people—and maybe people will have problems with them!

Moses had problems with people, so much so that one day he asked God to take his life because he'd had enough (Num. 11). Sometimes the people you help the most appreciate it the least. Jesus healed ten lepers, and only one of them—a foreigner—came back to thank Him (Luke 17:11–19). When Paul was a prisoner in Rome, some of the Roman Christians, instead of encouraging the apostle, tried to make things more difficult for him (Phil. 1:12–21). Paul took the loving approach and thanked God that at least they were preaching the gospel.

Ambrose Bierce wrote, "There are two classes of people: the righteous and the unrighteous. The classifying is done by the righteous." His satirical pen makes a significant point: sometimes we *create* problems with people because we adopt a "we/they" attitude. Everybody in the church (or Bible class or choir or youth group) is either for us or against us.

Most people think of a heretic only as somebody who teaches false doctrine. But the word translated "heresy" in the New Testament comes from a Greek word that means "to choose." It describes an office seeker campaigning for votes and asking everybody, "Are you for me or against me?" There's a willfulness about this attitude that often causes bad feelings and might produce division. If we take the "we/they" approach, we may become heretics; and instead of solving the problem, we will only make it worse.

You and I don't have to manufacture unity in the church because it's already there. We're all one in Christ (Gal. 3:28), and the spiritual oneness of the body is a miracle of God's grace (Eph. 4:1–6). No, we don't have to manufacture unity; but we do have the obligation to *maintain* the unity that Jesus died to create—"endeavoring to keep the unity of the Spirit in the bond of peace" (Eph. 4:3). So important is the unity of His people that Jesus prayed about it before He went to the cross (John 17:22–24).

If among God's people there's a difference over fundamental Bible doctrine, "the faith which was once for all delivered to the saints" (Jude 3), there can be no room for compromise. But let's be sure it's *fundamental* doctrine and not some secondary matter that somebody has blown out of proportion. For centuries, good and godly people have disagreed over the interpretations of certain Scriptures and have agreed to disagree without being disagreeable. "In essentials, unity; in non-essentials, liberty; in all things, charity." Augustine said that, and he's right.

That third statement from Augustine is especially important: "In all things, charity." Even when we defend the faith, we must behave like Christians: "And a servant of the Lord must not quarrel but be gentle to all, able to teach, patient, in humility correcting those who are in opposition, if God perhaps will grant them repentance, so that they may know the truth" (2 Tim. 2:24–25). If they don't repent, they're the ones who have broken the unity and left the fellowship (1 John 2:18–23). False doctrines cause divisions, and false teachers must be warned and avoided (Rom. 16:17–20).

But it's been my experience that very few ministries divide over doctrine. Most differences among Christians center on personalities, methods of ministry, allocation of funds, and other noteworthy but nondoctrinal matters. Let a church receive a large bequest from a will, and the potential for division is astronomical. The trustees want to use the money to pave the parking lot. The Missions Committee wants to send it to the fields. The women want to renovate the kitchen, and the young people want to build a gym. Not only is *loving* money a root of all kinds of evil, but *spending* it can produce a good deal of evil.

When in 1650 the General Assembly of the Church of Scotland opposed Oliver Cromwell and declared Charles II their king, Cromwell wrote them a letter of earnest appeal in which he said, among other things, "I beseech you, in the bowels of Christ, think it possible you may be mistaken."[1] *Appeal must precede attack if we are to act like Christians.* The army of Israel was commanded to offer peace to a city before declaring war against it (Deut. 20:10–20), and that's a good example for us to follow. Jesus instructed us to settle differences with people quickly and privately and to take the initiative in seeking peace (Matt. 5:21–26; 18:15–35).

The big problem, of course, is that we all think we have the right answer, and we're prepared to defend our "convictions." And when you add the implied threats that often accompany our "discussions" ("If you don't do this, our family will leave the church, and a lot of people will follow us!"), you have the potential for a real explosion. When that happens, it's time to sit down together and read aloud in unison Philippians 2:1–18. The next step is to suggest a prayer meeting to ask God to help everybody obey what was just read.

I have in my study a small sign a friend made for me when he heard me quote in a sermon a favorite statement from Thomas Merton. Here's the statement:

> To consider persons and events and situations only in the light of their effect upon myself is to live on the doorstep of hell.[2]

If Merton is right, a lot of Christians are sitting on a hot seat because they expect everybody to agree with them and everything to go their way. Like Lucifer, they insist on being "like the Most High" (Isa. 14:14) and playing God in everybody's life. The name of the malady is *pride*, and it's a difficult disease to cure.

New Testament scholar William Barclay wrote, "Pride is

the ground in which all the other sins grow, and the parent from which all the other sins come."[3] Among the sins that God hates most, pride heads the list (Prov. 6:16–17). The trouble is, sometimes pride masquerades as religious zeal; and the most bigoted believers can be mistaken for devoted defenders of the faith and crusaders for the cause of Christ.

God's servants don't always have to be right. Even Paul was occasionally perplexed about the will of God (Acts 16:6–10; 2 Cor. 4:8). When other people don't see things your way, trust God to show them what's right (Phil. 3:15). And be sure to ask God to show you if perhaps you may be wrong!

I once heard A. W. Tozer say, "Never be afraid of honest criticism. If the critic is wrong, you can help him; and if you're wrong, he can help you. Either way, somebody's helped."

Those of us who minister *for* Christ should strive to minister *like* Christ. He washed the feet of twelve men who were unworthy of His presence, let alone His service. He received and helped multitudes of people, many of whom never accepted His message. He died for a world that doesn't want Him. Why did He do it? Because it was the Father's will, and Jesus delighted to do His Father's will (Ps. 40:8).

And keep in mind that while you're serving others, the Lord is serving you. He's working with you on earth (Mark 16:20) and equipping you from heaven (Heb. 13:20–21). No matter how painful or disappointing your service may seem to you, *it's not being wasted.* God is building your character while He is building His church, and what He does will last forever. That makes even the criticisms worthwhile!

12

*D*uring my seminary days, I got acquainted with Noel O. Lyons, who was then executive director of Greater Europe Mission (GEM). Noel kept contact with me and my wife after we graduated and did his best to enlist us as missionaries to Germany. He was very persuasive, but the Lord had other plans for us.

I asked Noel one day, "How do you go about evaluating the missionary candidates who apply to GEM?" He explained their candidate program and then added, "I won't send a missionary to the field who doesn't have a sense of humor. No matter how much training and ability candidates may have, without a sense of humor, they may not make it on the field."

People who oppose humor among Christians have usually confused being *serious* with being *solemn*. "God cannot be solemn," wrote columnist Sidney Harris, "or he would not have blessed man with the incalculable gift of laughter."[1] The

Puritans are usually caricatured as stern and humorless, but it was Puritan preacher Richard Baxter who advised, "Keep company with the more cheerful sort of the godly; there is no mirth like the mirth of believers."[2]

I'm grateful that God gave me a sense of humor. If there's no laughter in heaven, I may ask for in-and-out privileges and find a planet where people laugh. Paradoxical as it sounds, laughter is serious business. Even Freud wrote a book entitled *Jokes and Their Relation to the Unconscious.* If you want to know what people are really like, find out what makes them angry, what makes them weep, and what makes them laugh. The test isn't infallible, but you'd be surprised how much it reveals.

A sense of humor is important in Christian service for several reasons. For one thing, being able to laugh at yourself and your situation helps to keep you balanced when you've made a mistake or when things fall apart. People who can laugh have a healthy sense of perspective about themselves and their work. Sure, they take it all seriously, but not so seriously that they think God will go out of business because they failed in something. Laughter isn't an escape from reality; it's evidence that we understand reality and can cope with it.

But laughter is also the lubricant that helps people work better together. One of the things that attracted me to Youth for Christ in those early days was the way the workers could be laughing uproariously one minute and then go to their knees weeping and praying the next minute; *and the laughing was just as serious to them as the praying.* I've seen humor defuse tension in a board meeting and free the people up to be themselves and go on with the meeting.

Someone has defined a *humorist* as "a person who can see more than one thing at a time." The ability to join together in your mind the things that other people put asunder, and then laugh about the combination, puts you at the head of the class. Creative people usually have a good sense of humor and know how to control it.

But humor is taboo whenever we're handling what is holy. You don't turn the Bible into a joke book and become what Phillips Brooks called "a clerical jester." I recall a preacher who introduced his sermon with a series of jokes about funerals. I groaned inwardly because in the congregation was a woman whose husband had committed suicide just a few weeks before. The preacher was surprised when very few people laughed. In serving the Lord, there's often a place for wit but rarely for comedy.

The ability to laugh at the right time and for the right reason is a gift from God that will do you more good than piles of pills and tons of therapy. A merry heart is still good medicine (Prov. 17:22), the gospel is still *good* news, and God still gives to His children "richly all things to enjoy" (1 Tim. 6:17). But our laughter must be the kind that strengthens us to face life honestly, not the kind that detours us from responsibility. Laughter and tears often go together. They don't cancel each other: they balance and enrich each other and work together to keep us sensible.

Mark Twain was wrong when he wrote in *Following the Equator*, "There is no humor in heaven." If there were no humor in heaven, there would be no humor on earth because we're made in the image of God. Somewhere C. S. Lewis wrote that "joy is the serious business of heaven." I vote with Lewis.

If the Lord ever stops laughing at the nations in revolt (Ps. 2:4) and starts beholding our stuffy business meetings and solemn assemblies, He will laugh even harder. If we aren't laughing with Him, something's wrong with us.

"Christian joy is a deeply serious thing," wrote Charles R. Bridges in his classic commentary on Proverbs. "Gloom is not the portion, and ought not to stamp the character, of the children of God."[3] I agree with him. We must cultivate a holy sense of humor as we busy ourselves with the most serious work on earth. Jesus was a "man of sorrows," but He left us a legacy of joy (John 17:13); and we ought to be investing it.

13

"*I*'ve had twenty-one years' experience in serving the Lord," a man proudly announced at a conference.

My friend sitting next to me whispered in my ear, "He's really had three years' experience seven times. He changes ministries so much that he rubber-stamps his name on the stationery."

Granted, some folks are bridge builders. They stay just long enough in a place to clear out the debris and get things ready for the next worker. But whether you're a pastor, a church officer, or a camp counselor, there's something noble and enriching about "staying by the stuff" and seeing things through. That kind of attitude is not only good for the work, it's also good for the worker because staying with the job helps you grow and get ready for the next job.

For years, I've kept under the glass on my desk a quotation that I clipped from a newspaper years ago. The clipping is faded now, but the message is still clear: "Make every occasion a great occasion, for you can never tell when someone may be taking your measure for a larger place." The quote is attributed to somebody named Marsden—no first name—so I can't tell you where to find it. But I'm sure glad *I* found it and can pass it along to you.

Marsden's quotation would make a good text for a sermon. If I used it that way, I'd probably say that it contains at least four implications: (1) our work is supposed to make us grow; (2) we're always being measured; (3) each job prepares us for the next one; and (4) the Lord may move us when He sees we're ready. If I wanted a biblical text to back it up, I'd quote our Lord's statement in Matthew 25:21: "Well done, good and faithful servant; you were faithful over a few things, I will make you ruler over many things. Enter into the joy of your lord."

If our service for the Lord doesn't make us grow, two things may be true: either we're in the wrong place, or we have the wrong attitude toward the right place. Both are tragic. But being miserable in your place of Christian service doesn't necessarily indicate that you're in the *wrong* place, so don't be too quick to back out. God may have put you there for *your* good as well as for the good of the work. Maybe He has some unfinished business to accomplish in your life.

I'm a person who likes to be comfortable in what I'm doing. I don't like too many changes or surprises. My comfort zone isn't big, but it's well-protected. However, the Lord sees to it that my defenses are regularly knocked down. He doesn't want me to get too accustomed to the challenge or too comfortable with the work. If that happens, He knows I'll stop growing; and then my work will start to have the quality of a flea market leftover.

Decades ago, one of my relatives deliberately failed third grade because in fourth grade he had to write with ink. I wonder what he would have done if passing had meant having to learn to operate a computer? I confess that I resisted graduating from my beloved typewriter to the computer (I wouldn't even use an *electric* typewriter!), but I finally gave in. I'm glad I did, but the transition was difficult. Why? Because I learned more about myself than I did about the computer, and some of the things I learned disturbed me.

The difficulty of the task God gives us is one of His loving gifts for our maturity. American industrialist Henry Kaiser, whose factories turned out a ship every six days during World War II, used to say that "problems are only opportunities in work clothes." When the Lord sees me mentally wearing pajamas and a bathrobe, He starts shaking things so I'll change clothes and get to work. I need the work more than the work needs me. Christian service is supposed to make us grow, and it will if we're in the right place with the right attitude.

We're always being measured: God is measuring us, and people are measuring us. When it comes to measuring Christian service and servants, other people can make mistakes, and *we* can make mistakes. Most Christian workers are prone to think either more highly of themselves than they should (Rom. 12:3) or less highly. If we think too highly of ourselves, we'll get proud and start pushing our way into what we think is a more important place. If we think less highly, we'll get discouraged and want to quit. Both attitudes are wrong.

The Lord is the only One who can accurately measure both us and our work, *but He doesn't always tell us what He thinks.* Languishing in Herod's dungeon, John the Baptist was sure he'd been a failure (Matt. 11:1–19); and more than once, Moses wanted to quit because he was sure he couldn't stand another day of listening to the people complain. (A travel magazine reports a sign in an Athens, Greece, hotel that reads: "Visitors are expected to complain at the office between the hours of 9 and 11 A.M." Moses didn't need a sign. The people just did what comes naturally.)

When God wants to encourage you and let you know that you're measuring up, He sometimes prompts people just to say thanks. They might phone you, write you a letter, or perhaps thank you personally. Phillips Brooks kept a few letters he'd received from grateful parishioners and sometimes read them during difficult hours. I don't recommend you start either a fan club or a testimonial scrapbook, but do be thankful for honest expressions of gratitude and accept them humbly as from the Lord.

Sometimes the Lord encourages you with a very special answer to prayer. It's His way of saying, "I like what you're doing and what I'm seeing in your life." When it happens, you'll find yourself behaving like the Jews after their deliverance from the enemy:

We were like those who dream.
Then our mouth was filled with laughter,
And our tongue with singing (Ps. 126:1–2).

One word of caution: be prepared for a super attack from the enemy because the devil doesn't like it when God's people are encouraged.

Another evidence that you've been measured and approved by the Lord is the opening of new doors of opportunity. If you've been faithful with a few things, God will give you more things. Of course, that means more work; but God has measured you and is sure you can do it. Over the years, it's been exciting to watch faithful servants grow and expand in their ministry to the glory of God. It's one of the few rewards of old age.

The important thing is that we do our work and not waste too much time measuring ourselves. "[People] who do their best always do more, though they be haunted by the sense of failure," said Scottish minister George Morrison. "Be good and true; be patient; be undaunted. Leave your usefulness to God to estimate. He will see to it that you do not live in vain."[1]

I've covered two points of my "sermon" from Marsden's quotation: our work is supposed to make us grow, and we're always being measured. The third point is obvious: each job prepares us for the next one.

The Bible contains many illustrations of this principle. Joseph was faithful as a servant, so God promoted him to being the second ruler in Egypt. Joshua was faithful as Moses' helper, so God appointed him Moses' successor. David was faithful as a shepherd, and God made him king of Israel. Granted, most of us won't become powerful rulers; but the principle still applies: each job prepares us for the next job.

However, I must issue a warning at this point: God's servants must never use their assignments as temporary stepping-stones for something greater. There's no place in the Lord's work for "pyramid climbers" who are so anxious to get to the top that they forget that

exaltation comes neither from the east
Nor from the west nor from the south.
But God is the Judge:

He puts down one,
And exalts another (Ps. 75:6–7).

If you ever find yourself promoting yourself for a promotion, read the book of Esther and get acquainted with Haman. God wants us to be ambitious, but be sure it's *godly* ambition.

That leads me to my fourth point: the Lord may move us when He sees we're ready. I say "may" because sometimes He lets His workers remain where they are so He can do a special work in them and through them. The size of the work isn't necessarily the remarkable thing; it's the kind of work God wants accomplished that counts.

But don't get the idea that staying in one place of service for a long time is necessarily an easy thing to do, because it isn't. Most ministries are better off when new people come on the scene, open the windows, and let in a breath of fresh air. A Sunday school teacher or church officer can become an institution if he or she isn't careful. It takes a very special person to stay in the same ministry a long time and not stifle the creativity of others or hinder the changes that need to be made. You have to keep growing, and you must stay in touch with the new generation so you don't develop a smothering good-old-days outlook on things.

When it comes to moving His servants, God's plan is never wrong, and His timing is never off. Sometimes He moves us to a bigger place, but He may move us to a smaller place that we're supposed to make bigger. He may put us in a situation for which we feel totally unprepared and in which we aren't at all comfortable. So much the better; He's giving us room to grow.

I suggest you copy the Marsden quotation and put it where you can see it frequently. Better yet, memorize it, along with Matthew 25:21. The Lord has some exciting things planned for you, and you don't want to be caught unprepared.

14

I want to pick up on the theme of the last chapter and chat with you about knowing *when* and *how* to close a ministry and move on to something else. Not everybody is supposed to pastor the same church for thirty years or teach the "Young in Heart" Sunday school class for a lifetime. I know a man in his nineties who still sings in the church choir, but he's an exception. I hope he'll be smart enough to step out when his voice changes. Knowing when to move *and how to make the move* can add special joy to your Christian service; but hanging on too long, or making the move impulsively, can cause scars both in you and in the church.

Let's begin with the obvious fact that nobody except the Holy Spirit is indispensable in the Lord's work. The church was here before we came along and will continue long after we're gone. There are times when we nurture our egos by telling ourselves that folks can't get along without us; but in our saner moments, we admit that these thoughts are pure fantasy. During more than forty years of ministry, I've resigned from three churches and two parachurch ministries, as well as several boards, and the work not only goes right on but is doing better than when I was there! So much for being indispensable.

The second obvious fact is that, for the most part, the people we serve are prone to resist change and will plead with us to stay on the job. They do this not necessarily because of their great love for us or our great ministry to them but because they don't want to go through the hassle of looking for a replacement. (This generalization doesn't apply if there's somebody in the group who wants your job, or if you're a pastor and there's somebody who has a brother-in-law looking for a church.) "Don't rock the boat!" is the unofficial motto of many ministries that have long since lost both their compass and their rudder and are gradually sinking in a sea of complacent tranquillity.

"Oh, what are we going to do without you?" a church member moaned when I resigned from my first pastorate.

"Better" was my reply; and I was right.

When I resigned as general director of Back to the Bible, a radio listener wrote me a severe letter informing me that I was out of the will of God. (It always amazes me how God makes His will for my life so clear to other people when I often have to ponder the Word and struggle and pray to discover what He wants me to do.) In a gentle but candid reply, I pointed out that either I knew God's will or I didn't. If I did, I had to obey. If I didn't know God's will, I was a dangerous leader to have around, and the ministry would be better off without me. Either way, it was a wise thing for me to go. The Lord never led the listener to reply.

One reason many ministries shift into neutral when it comes to appointing new workers or electing new officers is that somebody new might upset the security of the status quo. People get accustomed to working with each other, they know the family secrets, and they don't like it when a newcomer asks, "Why are we doing it this way?" At a church board meeting, I once raised a question about how the Lord's Supper was being served; and you would have thought I had denied the blood atonement. Ministries with self-perpetuating boards are especially vulnerable. If they aren't careful, the members of those boards can gradually vote themselves into sanctified paralysis. When unity becomes uniformity, it's time for a blood transfusion.

It's a law of the Medes and Persians that we never resign when (1) we're tired and discouraged, (2) we aren't getting our way, and (3) we feel unappreciated and we're looking for some strokes.

Let's start with weariness and discouragement. More than one servant of God has regretted confusing a weary spirit with the Holy Spirit and, like Elijah (1 Kings 19), quitting and running away. *Discouragement and depression are two of Satan's chief devices for getting Christians on detours.* The saintly spiritual director François Fénelon rightly called discouragement "the despair of wounded self-love." If we were honest, we'd call it the same thing.

Whenever you're tired and ready to quit, take a nap, go for a brisk walk, or be alone for a day's retreat. Have lunch with a discerning friend and talk it out. Get a fresh perspective on yourself and your work before making a decision you may regret. Any important decision you make when you're not at your best is likely to be a wrong one, so be patient.

When it comes to disagreements, ministries are better off

without people who stay on the job only because they always have their way. I have lived long enough to be thankful for people who resisted some of my ideas and weren't afraid to tell me they thought I was wrong. Of course, if the disagreement involves a matter of doctrine or ethics, we must maintain our integrity; but let's be sure we don't use doctrine or ethics to cover up a selfish spirit or a stubborn will. Many an angry bigot has masqueraded as a religious crusader.

In the Lord's work, we belong to each other, and we need each other; and it's possible to disagree without being disagreeable. Nobody can claim to always know the will of God in every decision that has to be made. Even the great apostle Paul admitted that there were times when he was "perplexed, but not in despair" (2 Cor. 4:8). Only God is omniscient.

I can't prove it, but I have a feeling that discovering the will of God is something like putting a picture puzzle together. God sees the complete picture because He painted it. Nobody has all the pieces of the puzzle; but as we talk and pray and meditate on the Word, each of us fits a piece into the puzzle. Gradually, we start to see the whole picture. Wanting to have our own way is like forcing a puzzle piece into the wrong place. *It's dangerous to try to change a picture that God has already planned.*

Every Christian worker has to learn how to accept disagreement and defeat graciously and admit that others may be right. Christian service is something like a good marriage: you don't always get your own way, you learn how to compromise lovingly, and you never say, "I told you so," if your mate's ideas don't work out. There's a place for happy compromise so long as the integrity of the ministry isn't questioned.

When your best ideas are turned down, remember two things. First, if the Lord wants to expedite your ideas, and if you wait and pray, He'll start to change people's minds. "If in anything you think otherwise," Paul wrote to the Philippians, "God will reveal even this to you" (Phil. 3:15). Second, your ideas may come to fruition after you've moved out into a different ministry. I've seen some of my best ideas pounded right into the carpet only to be resurrected and expedited years later when I was no longer on the scene. It's amazing how much God can accomplish if His workers don't care who gets the credit.

That leads us straight to the third wrong motive for resigning: we feel unappreciated, and we're hoping our resignation will trigger a verbal ticker-tape parade.

Being human, we all need to be stroked. Doctors tell us that babies need to be touched to feel loved and secure. My guess is that most of us never really outgrow that need. As we mature, we appreciate a handshake, a smile, a hug, the verbal massage of a sincere compliment. Mark Twain said that he could live for days on one good compliment, and Paul urged church members to show gratitude to their leaders for the good work they do (1 Thess. 5:12–13). Appreciation is reasonable, biblical, and psychologically sound.

So, what do we do if we aren't appreciated? Or what's even worse, what do we do if somebody else gets the praise that really belongs to us? Thomas Fuller said that praise makes good people better and bad people worse, and I agree. But let me add that lack of praise can make good people bad if they aren't careful.

One calculated risk Christian workers must take is the possibility of being misunderstood and not appreciated. It happened to Moses, David, Jeremiah, Paul, and Jesus; and it will probably happen to you. If your only motive for service is to be recognized and thanked, you had better get prepared for a lot of disappointment. But if your motive is to please God and accomplish His will, what people say and do—or don't say and do—won't make a great deal of difference to you. The praise of God will last forever; testimonial dinners are soon forgotten.

This chat has gone on long enough. I have more to say, so we'll pick it up in the next chapter.

15

*H*ow do we know when it's time to step out and let somebody else take over? The answer to that question involves several elements that must be dealt with honestly.

Keeping in mind that God's concern is for the worker as well as for the work, you need to ask yourself, Where am I in my spiritual growth? Does God still have some work to do in my life? *When your service is the most difficult, God may be doing His deepest work in your life, so don't run away.* God uses you to build His work, but He also uses the work to build you as He prepares you for the next assignment as well as for eternal service in glory.

Don't misunderstand me. I'm not saying that you leave a ministry simply because it doesn't "do anything for you" any longer. That's pure selfishness, the stepping-stone attitude of the pyramid climbers of the world. What I'm saying is that you need to be honest with yourself and see if you're still growing; if you're not, the work will suffer. God kept Joseph in prison two years longer than he expected because He had some more preparation to do in that young man's life.

A pastor friend of mine felt uncomfortable after ten years of ministry in his church and was sure that the time had come to move. But no other doors opened, so he stayed; and that eleventh year was the most difficult he and his wife ever experienced. Then everything changed, and he and the congregation entered into the most fruitful years the church had ever known. Both pastor and people moved to a new level of maturity because they were patient with each other and waited for the Lord to work. God wanted my friend to move, but it was a move *up* in maturity and not *out* into another ministry.

The second element you must consider is the state of the work itself. Are the people you serve able to cope with change? Can they handle a time of transition when you won't be there to steady them? Are there still major group decisions to make or ministry opportunities to seize? Are you counseling with people whose problems are still unsolved? Have you planted some seeds that still need nurturing? These are only a few of the questions that a compassionate Christian worker must ask before handing in a resignation.

You may answer some of these questions with, "A new person can do it better"; and maybe you're right. It's not unusual for God to change His workers. One person plows, another sows, another waters, but all of them are doing God's work. Just be careful that your saying, "Somebody else can do it better," isn't an excuse for quitting or a veiled request for praise.

Sometimes it's wise to confer with a close associate and get another perspective on the situation. No two people see the same scene in the same way, nor do we always see ourselves in the right perspective. But don't talk to too many people; it will lead only to confusion. Some of them may talk to others, which is the last thing you want. Until you've made your decision in the will of God, keep your circle of confidants small, and let them be the people who mean the most to you. By all means, take your leaders into your confidence because you're under their authority. But talking too much about your plans may be evidence that you're really not too sure of yourself and you're searching for somebody to tell you what you *want* to hear.

Okay, you've waited on the Lord, prayed, and counseled with people you trust and to whom you are accountable, and you've decided that God wants you to make a change. But before you write that letter of resignation, wait on the Lord for some word from His Word. No, you don't open your Bible at random and point to a verse. I'm talking about a special word from God *in the course of your regular daily Bible reading.* Or it may come in the course of regular worship. You'll know that God is speaking to you because the Holy Spirit will make some Scripture vivid and real to you in a way that simply can't be ignored.

I've already told you about my experience with God's promise in my first church building program. Let me tell you about the way the Lord spoke to me a few years later when I was about to start a building program in my second pastorate. It was to be a million-dollar project, and a million dollars was a lot of money in those days. (It's still a lot of money but not in many church building programs.)

The family and I were on our way to Wisconsin for a vacation, and we stopped in Chicago where I was to preach at a church pastored by a friend of mine. During the Sunday school hour, a gospel team from a Christian school ministered to the adult department; I was disappointed because I wanted to hear a Sunday school lesson from the Scriptures. The young man who spoke was above average in zeal but lacking in knowledge. However, his text so gripped me that I couldn't escape. Don't ask me what the young preacher said, because I don't remember; but I can give you his text:

> But none of these things move me; nor do I count my life dear to myself, so that I may finish my race with joy, and the ministry which I received from the Lord Jesus, to testify to the gospel of the grace of God (Acts 20:24).

I can't tell you how God spoke to me from that verse, not only during the Sunday school hour, but for the next two weeks as I was vacationing. God told me to stay where I was and to finish the job He sent me to accomplish in our church. I stayed, and God did some great things for us, undeserving as I was.

So, before you make that final decision, give the Lord time to talk to you from His Word. He may do it at the very beginning of your struggle to determine His will, or He may wait until later; but speak to you He will if you really want to know His will (John 7:17). Your experience may be something like that of Jacob when he was considering leaving Laban and going back to Bethel. Everything pointed to departure: the circumstances around him, the attitudes of people, and his own desires within; but Jacob waited for God's voice.

> Now Jacob heard the words of Laban's sons, saying, "Jacob has taken away all that was our father's, and from what was our father's he has acquired all this wealth." And Jacob saw the countenance of Laban, and indeed it was not favorable toward

him as before. Then the LORD said to Jacob, "Return to the land of your fathers and to your family, and I will be with you" (Gen. 31:1–3).

At the right time, God's word came to Jacob and told him what to do. But Jacob made a big mistake: he obeyed the word of God *but didn't do it in the right way.* Instead of trusting God and telling his father-in-law what God wanted him to do, Jacob got his clan together and quietly stole away. God gave Jacob a great opportunity to bear witness, but he preferred to get away while the getting was good. But that's not the way a believer says good-bye.

How you leave a place of service is just as important as knowing that God wants you to go. When God is truly in the decision and you've bathed it all in prayer, though a transition is painful, it is successful to the glory of God. The Holy Spirit lubricates the machinery, and the work goes on.

To begin with, your attitude ought to be positive and not negative. God isn't taking something away; He's opening the door to do something new. That doesn't mean you can't look back because a transition time can be a good testimony time when you let people know what God has done for you. But your attitude ought to be "hats off to the past and coats off to the future."

It's also a good time to say thanks to the people who have helped you and to tell them that their new leader deserves the same kind of loving support. Even if you don't fully agree with your successor, make it easy for the individual to take command. Don't be a party to any undercover resistance movements; and once you leave, don't hover or meddle. Treat your successor the way you want your predecessor to treat you when you move to a new ministry because you'll eventually reap what you sow.

16

John Rutter is one of my favorite musicians. Listening to his "Requiem" is to me a worship experience, and hearing his settings of the Psalms lifts my spirit in praise.

My wife and I attended a "Rutter Conducts Rutter" concert at which the noted composer/conductor did a strange thing. After the applause had ceased following a choral number, John Rutter turned to the audience and said, "Do you mind if we do that one again? I think we can do better." I was stunned. The first performance seemed excellent to me, but the ear of the gifted conductor heard something that the rest of us missed. The choir sang the song again, and Mr. Rutter seemed pleased.

More than once, I've wished I could turn to the congregation after the benediction and say, "Would you mind if I preached that sermon again? I think I can do better." I doubt that our congregations will start approving sermonic instant replays; but if we did, it would certainly relieve the preacher's conscience and remove that smothering feeling of disappointment that we all carry when we feel we haven't done our best.

In your particular place of service, the problem may not be the memory of a bad sermon. Maybe it's knowing that you taught a boring Sunday school lesson despite hours of painful preparation. Or perhaps you conducted a tedious committee meeting that accomplished nothing except to convince the committee members not to be committee members anymore. I'm sure church musicians wince when they recall some performances, and dedicated missionaries must have pages in their diaries that are stained with tears.

Which leads us to the overwhelming question: What do Christian workers do when they feel like they've done a poor job of serving the Lord?

If you and I were counseling somebody else about this matter, we'd probably say in a philosophical tone, "Well, you've got to remember that you learn more from your failures than you do from your successes." I like Charlie Brown's reply to that platitude: "That makes me the smartest person in the world!" Frankly, I'd rather learn from other people's failures. It doesn't cost me as much.

How do we learn from our failures? Not by sitting in a corner and brooding over them. That approach only prepares the way for another downfall. The smart thing to do is to evaluate what we did and try to find out what went wrong. Was it lack of preparation that routed us? Were we not at our best physically? Did we have a bad attitude that poisoned us? Was our spiritual preparation neglected? Were we overconfident?

There's a danger here that you must avoid. Don't spend so much time on this "autopsy" that you start bleeding to death emotionally and perhaps spiritually. Enough is enough. Honest self-examination is one thing, but brutal introspection only opens the way for the devil to start accusing you. No matter what you did wrong, confess it to the Lord and claim His forgiveness. Don't sit around recuperating—get busy! Someone has defined *failure* as "the path of least persistence," so get back to work as soon as possible. That's a part of the healing process.

Perhaps the hardest lesson we learn from failure is that we aren't as great as we thought we were. We're human, and creatures of clay have feet of clay and occasionally fall. Even Babe Ruth didn't hit a home run every time he was at bat. Failure has a way of humbling us, but we've got to be sure we're experiencing true humility and not just punctured pride. Punctured pride says, "How could this have happened *to me?*" while true humility says, "I'm surprised this doesn't happen more often."

Something else is involved: your ministry may look like a failure to you and yet be used by God to help somebody. I think it was Spurgeon who was lamenting preaching a poor sermon only to discover that two people were saved as a result of his message. Had they never told him, he would have considered his efforts a failure. Of all the books I've published, the one I think is the poorest written and contains the weakest exposition is the one that has sold the most copies! Who am I to argue with my public?

Do your work by faith, and leave the results with the Lord. Always strive to do your best; but if you do occasionally strike out, don't sit on the bench feeling sorry for yourself. Get ready for the next time at bat!

17

*T*his chat is for Christian workers who are classified as senior citizens by the younger crowd.

It was once my privilege to be the pastor of a man who died at the age of ninety-four. He had hoped to make it to the century mark, and we were all rooting for him; but the Lord had other plans. My wife and I often visited him in his apartment where he'd make dinner for us (he was a good cook), and we'd sit and talk about his future plans. We rarely heard good-old-days conversation when we were with him. He was always looking ahead.

"You're only as young as your mind," he said one day. "I consider myself a young man." So did his friends. He outlived a couple of doctors and accountants, and he told me he had to keep making younger friends or he'd find himself lonely. We felt privileged to be counted among his younger friends. I guess when a man is in his nineties, most of his friends would be younger.

I asked him one day why he hadn't moved into a retirement home. He was offended.

"What?" he almost shouted. "Move in with a bunch of old people who do nothing but play with trains and sit around and talk about their symptoms? Not on your life!" I never brought up the subject again, although I think his description was prejudiced and highly exaggerated.

He never lost his sense of humor. The night before he was to have surgery, his surgeon said to him, "I want you to know that this operation is serious." My friend replied, "Doctor, at my age, *a haircut is serious!*" He made it through the surgery and enjoyed a few more years of getting old but living young. I often think of him, and his memory encourages me.

The older we get and the longer we serve the Lord, the more we need to work at being contemporary and not becoming dusty relics in a religious museum. We may retire from a *vocation,* but we must never retire from *life.* God wants us to be players, not spectators, even though we may not be first string anymore. Even King David came to a time in his life when he had to put up his sword and leave the battles to the younger men (2 Sam. 21:15–17).

We have to work at being contemporary because nobody automatically stays young in heart and mind. Much that's within me and a great deal of what's around me have conspired to make me *feel* old and *think* old and *act* old. But living old is a choice we make; it isn't an inevitable sentence from Mother Nature and Father Time. "To me," said Bernard Baruch, "old age is always fifteen years older than I am." I like his outlook.

If you want to live in the past and criticize the present, especially the younger generation, you're free to do so; but you'd better weigh the consequences. Remember the word

Erinaceus that I introduced in our fourth chat? It describes what will happen to you if you let yourself become old. You'll become like that hedgehog, and nobody will want to risk getting near you. Gradually you'll become isolated, critical, bitter, and desperate in your feeble attempt to bring back the past and resist the present. Of course, that's an ideal way to destroy the future.

I may be wrong, but I have a feeling that the younger generation doesn't ignore or oppose senior saints because we're older or because we don't agree on everything. When it comes to the younger leaders God is raising up in the church, and the new things He's doing, we senior saints have a tendency to react instead of respond, to talk instead of listen, and to build walls instead of bridges. *And I believe that the motivation behind these reactions is fear, especially the fear that we older folks won't be needed anymore.*

"We do not count a man's years," wrote Emerson, "until he has nothing else to count."

That's a sad statement, but I fear it's true. *No matter how old you are, count for something, even if it's only that you listen to the younger crowd, pray for them, and encourage them to live for God.* You may have to reluctantly resign from the board or from some church activity, but don't resign from serving the Lord. And please don't go underground, mobilize the old-timers, and create problems for your pastor by opposing everything new in the church program. Remember the statement from Thomas Merton that I quoted in the eleventh chat? It says,

> To consider persons and events and situations only in the light of their effect upon myself is to live on the doorstep of hell.

The doorstep of hell is a terrible place to retire!

What I've said so far must not be interpreted as encouraging senior saints to develop a laissez-faire attitude toward the next generation. We have responsibilities to fulfill toward them, and the Lord will hold us to it. In case you've forgotten, here are a few things that the Lord expects of the older generation:

The silver-haired head is a crown of glory,
If it is found in the way of righteousness
(Prov. 16:31).

That the older men be sober, reverent, temperate, sound in faith, in love, in patience; the older women likewise, that they be reverent in behavior, not slanderers, not given to much wine, teachers of good things (Titus 2:2–3).

Come, you children, listen to me;
I will teach you the fear of the LORD (Ps. 34:11).

Now also when I am old and grayheaded,
O God, do not forsake me,
Until I declare Your strength to this generation,
Your power to everyone who is to come (Ps. 71:18).

I will open my mouth in a parable;
I will utter dark sayings of old,
Which we have heard and known,
And our fathers have told us.
We will not hide them from their children,
Telling to the generation to come the praises of the LORD,
And His strength and His wonderful works that He has done. . . .
That the generation to come might know them,
The children who would be born,
That they may arise and declare them to their children,

That they may set their hope in God,
And not forget the works of God,
But keep His commandments;
And may not be like their fathers,
A stubborn and rebellious generation,
A generation that did not set its heart aright,
And whose spirit was not faithful to God (Ps. 78:2–4, 6–8).

In these Scriptures, God tells us to be an encouragement to the younger folks so they won't make the mistakes we made. We're supposed to teach them what's right by our example and our encouragement. *Every local church is but one generation short of extinction.* A church composed only of elderly people will soon be a cemetery, but a church made up only of young people may lack the balance that comes from mature counsel. Give it enough time, and it may destroy itself.

When they wrote the words I've just quoted, I don't think David, Solomon, Asaph, and Paul were thinking only about formal instruction in a classroom. The Jews were accustomed to discussing God's truth in the informal situations of life (Deut. 6:6–9), a good example for us to follow. The important thing is that we senior saints listen sympathetically to the younger generation so they'll be willing to listen to us. If warning is needed, we must give it; but (to use Spurgeon's phrase) let's not walk around with a revolver in our pocket and do nothing but look for targets.

It's our job to prepare the younger generation to step in and take over. If they fail, we may blame them; but it may be our fault because we didn't train them better. "And the things that you have heard from me among many witnesses, commit these to faithful men who will be able to teach others also"

(2 Tim. 2:2)—Paul had four generations of Christians in mind when he wrote that, pretty good vision for a senior saint!

Once we've handed the torch to the next generation, we must avoid committing two blunders. The first is "hovering and meddling" and robbing our successor of the freedom to do what needs to be done. The second blunder is imitating Pontius Pilate and washing our hands of everything, thereby abandoning our years of experience instead of investing them when they are needed. Somewhere in between is the right posture, and the Lord can help us find it.

One of the joys of senior saints is to keep our eyes open to find new recruits for the kingdom of God. We can challenge them, help to train them, and then encourage them to do the job, making ourselves available when they need our help. As I get older, I find great joy in seeing the way God is blessing some of the young men and women He helped me influence in past years, as students in the classroom, as staff members, as members of the church, or simply as friends.

The younger generation isn't just the future *of* the church. It's the future *in* the church *right now*, and we dare not ignore it. Read again the Scriptures I quoted earlier. Then ask God to help you put them to work right where you are today.

18

Now it's time to chat with the younger workers. I've got to be fair all around.

Someone asked the American historian Charles A. Beard if he could summarize the lessons of history in a brief book. He said he could do it in four sentences: "(1) Whom the gods would destroy, they first make mad with power; (2) The mills of God grind slowly, but they grind exceeding small; (3) The bee fertilizes the flower it robs; (4) When it is dark enough, you can see the stars."[1]

I can summarize in four sentences what I want to say to my younger friends serving the Lord:

1. Never take down a fence until you know why it was put up.
2. If you get too far ahead of the army, your soldiers may mistake you for the enemy.
3. Don't complain about the bottom rungs of the ladder; they helped to get you higher.

4. If you want to enjoy the rainbow, be prepared to endure the storm.

My list may not be as profound as Beard's, but I wish somebody had shared it with me forty years ago.

19

Readers are leaders.

That statement is probably a cliché, but it's still true; and I hope you believe and practice it. If you do, you can stay ahead of the pack and reach your goals a lot easier and a lot faster. And while you're at it, you'll find yourself maturing in a balanced way that will honor the Lord and make you a more effective worker.

Your heart grows by giving out, but your mind grows by taking in; and both are necessary to a happy and balanced life of service. Christian workers who don't read aren't taking in fuel for the mind and food for the soul, and they end up trying to spin out their ministry like a spider's web. Bees have a much better approach. They gather pollen from many sources but manufacture their own honey. Most people prefer honey to spiders' webs.

Several myths about reading ought to be exposed, slain, and interred once and for all. The first is that you have to be "the student type" to be an effective reader. I don't know how many times I've heard Christian workers say, "Well, that's okay for you because you're a bookworm. But I'm just not the student type."

I don't mind being called a worm—even a bookworm—because my Lord called Himself a worm when He hung on the cross for me (Ps. 22:6); but I'm not sure I know what "the student type" is. I suppose these people are referring to the ivory-tower scholar who always has his nose in a book and his feet firmly planted in the air, the pseudointellectual who avoids responsibility by haunting the halls of academe while he slowly dies by degrees. If that's the case, I don't qualify, and I'm glad.

But if by "the student type" they mean somebody who loves truth and eagerly pursues it, who believes that all truth is God's truth, who knows that books are the treasure troves of the ages just waiting to be mined, I plead guilty. One of the qualifications for ministry is "able to teach" (1 Tim. 3:2), and it seems reasonable that "able to teach" implies "able to learn." Otherwise, what are you going to teach?

I've been told by some antireading advocates, "Jesus called His followers 'disciples' and not 'students,' so we need to be careful that we don't overdo this reading bit." If they understood the meaning of the word *disciple*, they'd see how weak that argument is. Perhaps the nearest thing we have to the word *disciple* is *apprentice*, someone who lives with a master workman, watches him, and learns from him, and then puts what he learns into practice under the watchful eye of the teacher. What he learns, he's able to share with others because he's done it himself. Reading is a part of our apprenticeship with the Lord; it's one way He teaches us.

Except for some eccentric anti-intellectual sects that

equate ignorance with sanctity, the Christian faith has always emphasized the importance of learning as a tool for living. God gave us an inspired Book to read, and we preach sermons from it, write books about it, support scholars to study it, and establish churches and schools to teach it. Whether you accept it or not, if you're a part of the Christian church, you're a part of a community that for centuries has emphasized education as well as training.

When you stop reading, you stop growing; and when you stop growing, you start dying. The process may be slow and painless, but the paths on which the nonreader walks lead but to the grave.

But let me hasten to slay another myth, namely, that reading books will *of itself* guarantee growth and success. Not so. Reading is only the key that opens the door to the vault. *Assimilating* what you read, *relating* it to what you already know, and *practicing* it where you serve put the treasure to work paying dividends. It's tragic to open the vault and stand there empty-handed. Readers are leaders only if they turn their learning into living. To change the metaphor, reading a book is like eating a meal; but if you eat and don't exercise, you'll get overweight, and you may die.

The words of Thomas à Kempis apply here: "Truly on the day of judgment we shall not be examined on what we have read, but what we have done; not how well we have spoken, but how religiously we have lived."[1]

A third dragon I need to slay is the idea that you have to read *many* books, especially the best-sellers, to qualify as a good reader. Publishers and booksellers feed this dragon because it frightens people into buying new books, whether they read them or not. These worried customers purchase all the best-sellers only to put them on the shelf, always promising themselves to get around to reading them. When a book title comes up in conversation, they can always say, "Yes, I have that; but I haven't had a chance to finish it yet." Having read the blurbs on the dust jacket, they can bluff their way through any discussion. The books might as well be back in the store as far as they're concerned; they're getting no good out of them at all.

When you call a book a best-seller, you're not necessarily saying that it's the best book on the subject or even that it's a good piece of literature. *Best-seller* is a term coined in 1895 by the editor of *The Bookman*, Harry Thurston Peck, simply to identify books that sell the best. It's entertaining to browse through Alice Payne Hackett's *70 Years of Best Sellers (1895–1965)* and discover titles of books that in their day were famous but have long since been forgotten, such as *Sparkenbroke* (1936), *And Tell of Time* (1938), and *Top Secret* (1946). Daniel J. Boorstin called a best-seller "a celebrity among books . . . a book known primarily (sometimes exclusively) for its well-knownness."[2] He ought to know; he was librarian of the Library of Congress for a dozen years.

Hard on the heels of the best-seller myth comes the myth of the big library. Many preachers and Bible teachers fervently believe this myth, and the people who live with them and trip over their ever-expanding library just as fervently abominate it. The argument is mathematical: if one book on the gospel of John makes you smart, twenty books on the gospel of John will make you twenty times smarter.

I just did a head count in my library and discovered that I have over fifty volumes devoted to the gospel of John. (I didn't include one-volume commentaries on the whole Bible.) But if God ordered me to cut that down to a dozen books, I think I could do it and probably not weaken either my library or my ministry. I'm glad I have that many volumes on John's gospel because they've all helped me in one way or another, but I must confess that I haven't used some of them for years.

A library should be a *collection* and not just an accumulation of books, a gourmet meal and not a potluck dinner. I don't know about you, but I have neither the money to purchase nor the time to read every book published on any given subject. What busy preachers or Bible teachers have the time to study fifty authors' statements about any given passage in the Bible? And if they do, it's still no guarantee that reading them makes them better prepared for their ministry. The mechanic has a tool for every job, but what good is it to carry around ten tools for every job?

Now for a caveat: if you specialize in some area of study, your library will announce it. For more than a quarter century, I've specialized in Christian biography, which explains why there are nearly a thousand volumes in the biography section of my library. I've also majored on Victorian history and the preachers of that era, and I have a large collection of sermon books, which are all carefully indexed. I keep adding volumes to each of these collections because they're important to the work God has called me to do.

Myth number five is what I call the best-book myth. I frequently get letters or phone calls from people who want me to give them the names of the best books on a given topic. I know what the best books are for me, but I'm afraid I can't prescribe for everybody else. A book is a tool, and the hammer that's just right for me might be much too heavy for my four-year-old grandson. I once gave an associate a book that I found very useful, and a few years later he gave it back to me. His honest explanation was, "I don't know how to use it."

In the early years of my ministry, I had such high respect for Dr. Wilbur Smith that I used to buy many of the books he recommended, only to discover that not all the tools fit my hands. I still think highly of Dr. Smith, and I've benefited from many of his suggestions; but I quickly learned not to buy a book just because somebody said it was the best.

"The best book is not the one that informs merely," wrote A. W. Tozer, "but the one that stirs the reader up to inform himself."[3] The best book is the book that helps you live and do your best. Just as David couldn't fight wearing Saul's armor, so you and I can't work using tools that are designed for somebody else.

The sixth dragon to slay is the myth of the approved author. Both inside and outside the church, people with cultic minds keep this dragon very much alive. They have lists of authors who are "safe," "questionable," and "forbidden"; and they use their lists as tests of fellowship and spirituality. I heard of a pastor who took all of my titles out of his church bookroom because I endorsed a book written by a theologian he disagrees with. Apparently he's afraid I might corrupt his people, although I haven't written anything on the subject over which we disagree.

To be sure, we have to use discretion and common sense when we recommend books to young people and immature Christians. We don't ask them to chew on meat before they've grown some teeth. And when they are ready for the challenge, we have to caution them to exercise discernment; *but they'll be doing that the rest of their lives.* As we mature in Christ, we stop choosing between the good and the bad and start distinguishing the better and the best.

"Beware of the atmosphere of the classics," Robert Murray M'Cheyne wrote to a friend. "True, we ought to know them; but only as chemists handle poison—to discover their qualities, not to infect their blood with them."[4] He offered good counsel, and I recommend it to you. No matter who wrote the books you read, test what you read by the Word of God and hold on to "whatever things are true... noble...just...pure...lovely...of good report" (Phil. 4:8).

I urge you to read widely and learn everything you can from as many authors as possible. Reading is something like eating, and we all have different tastes. Some writers who excite my friends completely bore me, but that just means our appetites are different. Would you break fellowship with people who didn't enjoy Chinese food or pasta?

However, don't read so widely that you fail to zero in on authors who are really on your wavelength. Don't become a disciple of any author, no matter how much help the person gives you; but do get to know writers whose message makes you a better person, a better student, and a better servant of the Lord.

No matter how old a book may be, it's a new book to you if you've never read it, so dare to read authors who are new to you. Give yourself time to get acquainted; you might make a friend for life. One of the best ways to meet new authors is to read anthologies, old and new. To me, an anthology is a smorgasbord prepared by dozens of great cooks, and it's all mine to enjoy! You'll find them in your local library. I know: I've bought several of them at library sales!

Even though Henry David Thoreau was many things I am not—a naturalist, a bachelor, a camper, a fisherman, a church dropout, and somewhat of a loner—his *Walden* is one of my favorite books and has accompanied me on many a trip. When I get to chapter 3—"Reading"—I usually find myself smiling and nodding in agreement. Mr. Thoreau writes,

> To read well, that is, to read true books in a true spirit, is a noble exercise, and one that will task the reader more than any exercise which the customs of the day esteem. It requires a training such as the athletes underwent, the steady intention almost of the whole life to this object. . . . How many a man has dated a new era in his life from the reading of a book.[5]

Maybe you're ready for that new era in *your* life.

20

I once heard Henrietta Mears, founder of Gospel Light Publications, say that she was not married for only one reason: the apostle Paul was dead.

But if she *had* been married, even to the great apostle Paul, I wonder if Miss Mears would have accomplished all that she did accomplish? We'll never know; but this much is sure: if you *are* married, you've got to take your mate and your children into consideration if you want to serve the Lord effectively. Otherwise you may end up destroying both your ministry and your marriage.[1]

"He who is unmarried cares for the things of the Lord—how he may please the Lord. But he who is married cares about the things of the world—how he may please his wife" (1 Cor. 7:32–33). Paul's statement sounds dogmatic and demanding; but when you read the context, you get a balanced perspective. Paul wasn't against people getting married or married people serving the Lord. He was against people getting married out of the will of God and ignoring "the present distress" (v. 26). Love may be blind, but Paul wanted the Christians in Corinth to get married with their eyes open.

Jesus taught that not everybody is supposed to get married (Matt. 19:10–12); but generally speaking, it's the best thing for most people. "It is not good that man should be alone" was God's assessment of the situation, and He provided the solution to the problem by instituting marriage. I can certainly bear witness to the fact that my wife has been an essential part of our ministry and that we were able to do what God called us to do because we're a team. Some very effective ministers have chosen to remain single, but I'm glad the Lord didn't call me to be one of them.

In marriage, "two become one," and this miracle must never be forgotten. Marriage means that a man and a woman must no longer say "mine" and "yours"; they should say only "ours." If one of them has a ministry, they both have a ministry, whether the other one accepts it or not. Marriage isn't a fifty-fifty partnership; it's a 100 percent stewardship in which each mate lives for the other and both live for the Lord.

A cursory reading of Paul's statement in 1 Corinthians 7:32–33 may give you the impression that married people have to choose between pleasing the Lord and pleasing their mate, but that's not the case at all. The apostle is simply saying, "If you do get married and you want to serve the Lord, *choose the kind of Christian mate who is pleased when you please the Lord.* Then there won't be any division in the home, and you can both serve God effectively."

Let me state it another way. When it comes to the relationship between ministry and marriage, if you ask enough people, you'll end up with three different philosophies. Some will tell you that the home must come first and the Lord's work take second place. Others will reverse that and insist that the ministry has priority over the home. I disagree with both approaches for two reasons: I don't think they're biblical, and they automatically create conflict.

If indeed "two become one," home and ministry are united; they are one. What God has joined together, we must not put asunder.

Since the ministry God gave me and my wife was primarily with local churches, let me use pastoral ministry to illustrate my point. What makes for a good church? At least three things: love, truth, and discipline. We speak the truth in love (Eph. 4:15) and practice the truth in loving discipline. What makes for a good home? Love, truth, and discipline. The Christian home and the Christian church are built with the same tools—the Word of God and prayer—and on the same foundation: love, truth, and discipline.

The best thing my wife and I could do for the churches we served was to build a good home and raise children that were a credit to the Lord and to the church. And the best thing we could do for our home was to build good churches for our children to attend. The two became one.

As long as the home and the church are being built with the same spiritual tools and on the same spiritual foundations, there ought to be no serious conflict. Conflict comes when we neglect love, truth, discipline, prayer, or the Word of God in the home or in the church. Conflict also comes when parents are one thing at home and quite something else at church. (The word for this is *hypocrisy*.) This situation creates confusion in the minds of our children and gives the enemy opportunity to move in.

When our children understand that everybody in the family is a part of the ministry, and that together we are all building the church and building our home, we have a common outlook to help us in making decisions. It isn't an either/or situation; it's both/and.

In our own ministry, there were times when the family schedule had to be adjusted because of needs in the congregation. But there were times when the best thing my wife and I could do for the church was to devote extra time to the family. In spite of complaining about the demands of ministry, the pastor makes his own schedule and has calendar privileges that other people in the church don't have. We made our share of mistakes (thank God for forgiving children!), but I don't recall that we felt like the family and the church were at war with each other.

The problems get more complicated when the children get older and start getting involved in piano lessons, sports, slumber parties, baby-sitting, part-time jobs, and all the other rites of passage that belong to modern life. That's when we all have to start practicing the give-and-take of managing the family circus, the first rule of which is, *nobody is always in the center ring.* Once we agree on that, things become easier.

I don't have to tell you that the machinery of the Christian home is lubricated by prayer. Dad and Mom must have their own personal devotional time every day, and they also need to lead the children in a family devotional time. Not a long religious routine, not a boring liturgy, but a brief (not hurried) look into the Word and a meaningful time of prayer.

Each family has to design its own approach, *and don't be afraid to laugh occasionally.* Few things will drive children away from the Bible and prayer like being forced to be happy while enduring a stuffy family devotional time. But praying with your family around the table will mean nothing if your children know you don't take time to pray in private, or if they know that you and your mate don't pray together. Truth, love, and discipline make the home Christian, but these things have to begin with Dad and Mom.

Regardless of the ministry you now have—full-time or volunteer—if your ministry is hurting your home, there's something wrong with your home or your ministry or both. God doesn't usually tear down one good thing to build up another good thing. If your home is competing with your ministry and creating uncomfortable friction, you need to stop and take stock of things and make some radical changes.

Remember, the best thing you can do for your ministry is build a godly family; and the best thing you can do for your family is build a ministry that glorifies God. Home and ministry are friends, not enemies; and it's your job to keep them that way.

21

*I*t's been my privilege on many occasions to preach at The People's Church in Toronto, Canada. Some years ago, I was sitting in the office of the founder, the late Dr. Oswald J. Smith, and we were discussing the photographs hanging on the wall.

"Who's that gentleman there?" I asked, pointing to a photograph. "It looks like somebody I should know."

"That's B. D. Ackley," said Dr. Smith, "the man who composed the music for nearly one hundred of my songs."

Do you happen to know the name of the first song that O. J. Smith and B. D. Ackley collaborated on?

"There's Joy in Serving Jesus."

There *is* joy in serving Jesus, no matter what kind of service He's called you to do. *Don't ever lose this joy.* If you do, your service will start to become a burden, and you'll feel like quitting. Why? Because "the joy of the LORD is your strength" (Neh. 8:10).

"Let us rejoice with one another," said Phillips Brooks, "that in a world where there are a great many good and happy things for men to do, God has given us the best and happiest, and made us preachers of His Truth."[1] Brooks was speaking to ministerial students, but the statement applies to any kind of Christian service. The "best and happiest" thing we can do is to serve the Lord.

The apostle Paul was a courageous man. He wasn't afraid to travel in dangerous places, face disagreeable people, or fight difficult enemies. But there was one thing that Paul feared, and he wasn't ashamed to admit it: "Lest, when I have preached to others, I myself should become disqualified" (1 Cor. 9:27).

The image comes from the Greek games. Paul saw himself as the official herald who announced the events, named the qualified contestants, and reminded them of the rules. That was Paul *the apostle*, enlisting others in the Christian race and encouraging them to obey the rules (2 Tim. 2:5). But he was also Paul *the believer*, running the race. He was fearful lest he be put out of the race because he hadn't obeyed the rules. It wasn't a matter of going to heaven because that was settled when he trusted the Savior. It was a matter of losing his ministry and the prize Jesus would give him at the end of the race (Phil. 3:12–16).

What would you do if God took your ministry away from you? Would you be relieved and start looking for something else to do? If so, it's possible you shouldn't be ministering in the first place. Would you calmly drop out of the race, become bitter, and turn your back on the Lord? Or would you seek His face and plead for the privilege of serving Him? I hope you would say, "I'd rather die and go to heaven than do anything that would grieve the Lord and make me lose my ministry!"

No matter what kind of Christian service God has called you to, *it's a privilege to be in ministry and to serve Jesus Christ.* In some ways, it's the hardest work in the world; but in many ways, it's the happiest work in the world. Yes, it has its tears and trials, but it also has its joys and triumphs; *and the best is yet to come!*

What are the joys involved in Christian service?

First and foremost, I think, is the joy of pleasing the Lord because you're doing what He wants you to do. God delights in His people, and it pleases His heart when His servants do His will from their hearts (Eph. 6:6). Pleasing God ought to be your supreme motive for service. If it is, you'll hear His "well done" when you stand before Him in glory (Matt. 25:21).

There's also the joy of growing more like the Master as you do His will. Every Christian ought to strive to become "conformed to the image of His Son" (Rom. 8:29), and those who serve Him have a wonderful opportunity to learn from Him and become more like Him. Remember what M'Cheyne wrote: "It is not great talents God blesses so much as great likeness to Jesus."[2]

There's a third joy, and that's the joy of helping others come to know Jesus Christ and live for Him. No matter what tasks He calls you to do, God will use them to help somebody if you do them in the power of the Spirit and for His glory. You may not even know about it! But you can trust your Father to see to it that nothing is ever wasted that is done in the will of God and for the love of God. Isn't that what Jesus told Mary when she anointed Him (John 12:1–8)?

That leads to a fourth joy, the joy of knowing that, as you serve the Lord, nothing happens to you except what God ordains. Paul wrote his most joyful letter while a prisoner in Rome awaiting possible execution. "But I want you to know, brethren, that the things which happened to me have actually turned out for the furtherance of the gospel," he wrote to his friends in Philippi (Phil. 1:12). Neither Paul's safety nor his comfort was the most important thing on his mind. The most important thing was that the gospel be proclaimed in Rome and that people turn to the Savior.

Another joy of ministry is the wonderful fellowship you have with other people who are serving God. Jesus promised His servants that they would have "brothers and sisters and mothers and children" (Mark 10:30), and He keeps that promise. What an enriching experience it is to belong to the fellowship of service and know that others are praying for you just as you are praying for them!

I could go on, but let me close with the joy of knowing that your service for Christ will last eternally: "He who does the will of God abides forever" (1 John 2:17). Most of the people you meet day after day are either wasting their lives or merely spending their lives, but God's servants have the privilege of *investing* their lives in what is eternal. The oft-quoted words of Jim Elliot say it perfectly: "He is no fool to give what he cannot keep to gain what he cannot lose."

In September 1948, I was a lonely young man just starting my seminary studies. As I sat in my dormitory room in the big city of Chicago, I asked the Lord to give me a verse that would assure and encourage me during the difficult years before me; and He answered that prayer. He gave me my life verse, Psalm 16:11:

You will show me the path of life;
In Your presence is fullness of joy;
At Your right hand are pleasures forevermore.

Life! Joy! Pleasures!
Who enjoys these priceless blessings? Those who walk on God's path, live in God's presence, and seek God's pleasures.
Those who serve the Lord.
Whatever happens, *don't lose the joy of serving Jesus!*

22

The official *Dictionary of Foreign Words*, issued in 1951 by the then Soviet government, describes the Bible as "a collection of different legends, mutually contradictory and written at different times and full of historical errors, issued by churches as a 'holy' book." We don't agree with that definition, but at least the people who wrote the dictionary thought the Bible important enough to deny that it is what it claims to be.

Whatever else we may be, we evangelical Christians are a people of the Book; and that Book is the Bible. We may not always practice what it teaches, but we'll defend the Bible with our last ounce of strength. To us, the Bible *is* a holy book, the "Holy Scriptures" (2 Tim. 3:15), inspired by the Holy Spirit and written by "holy men of God" (2 Pet. 1:21). And those of us who love it and study it ought to be living holy lives.

Dr. Will H. Houghton used to say, "Lay hold of the Bible until the Bible lays hold of you." Martin Luther went much further when he said, "The Bible is alive, it speaks to me; it has feet, it runs after me; it has hands, it lays hold on me."[1]

No matter what ministry the Lord has assigned to you, *you can't succeed apart from the Word of God.* Let me explain why.

To begin with, the Word of God reveals the God of the Word; and the servants must know the Master if we are to serve Him acceptably. We don't read the Bible to mark "precious promises," although hundreds of them are there; nor do we read the Bible to understand "Bible doctrine," although doctrine is essential. *We read the Bible to get to know the heart and mind of God.* The better we know God, the better we can enjoy Him and minister for Him.

"How can I know the will of God?" is best answered by, "Get to know the character of God." God never acts in violation of His character, and that character is revealed in the Bible. Too many Christians think that God tolerates sin the way most people do, and that the absence of His discipline means the approval of their disobedience. Not so! "You thought that I was altogether like you," warned God, "but I will rebuke you" (Ps. 50:21).

For too long a time, I saw the Bible as a devotional guide, a theology text, and a sourcebook for sermons. It was not a living link between me and God. What a difference it made when I began to pray what I had sung so many times:

Beyond the sacred page,
I seek Thee, Lord.
My spirit pants for Thee,
O living Word.[2]

"The essence of idolatry," wrote A. W. Tozer, "is the entertainment of thoughts about God that are unworthy of him."[3] But if we're to have *worthy* thoughts about God, and therefore live and serve in ways worthy of Him, we must spend time reading His Word. We need to cultivate the attitude of Jeremiah, who wrote,

> Your words were found, and I ate them,
> And Your word was to me the joy and rejoicing of my heart;
> For I am called by Your name,
> O LORD God of hosts (Jer. 15:16).

The Word of God reveals the character of God to us, and as it does, it also renews the mind so that we start to think the way God wants us to think: "And do not be conformed to this world, but be transformed by the renewing of your mind, that you may prove what is that good and acceptable and perfect will of God" (Rom. 12:2).

One of the dangers in ministry is that we start thinking the way the world thinks and then doing things the way the world does them (Ps. 1:1–3). To be sure, the children of this world can teach us some things (Luke 16:8); but note that their counsel is limited to "their generation" and doesn't touch the eternal.

> For as the heavens are higher than the earth,
> So are My ways higher than your ways,
> And My thoughts than your thoughts (Isa. 55:9).

What works for IBM or General Motors may not succeed in the local church.

Evangelist D. L. Moody used to say that "some people are so heavenly minded they're no earthly good." That's not what Romans 12:2 and Colossians 3:1 are talking about. To have "the mind of Christ" means to look at things from our Lord's perspective, to look at earth from heaven's point of view. It means to be prepared for the unusual, even the impossible. The "renewed mind" sees life as it really is and doesn't get fooled by the false diagnoses of the blind optimistic physicians who reject the Word of God.

Ministry is something that we do by faith, and "faith comes by hearing, and hearing by the word of God" (Rom. 10:17). "According to your faith let it be to you" is still God's way of working (Matt. 9:29); and the measure of our faith is the result of quality time spent in the Word of God. Unless what we do is based on what God says and what God is, we will find ourselves failing. What we thought was faith was really only sentimental presumption. We were not trusting God; we were tempting God.

I recall being in the board meeting of a fine Christian ministry as the directors discussed a tough budget problem. "I think we should just launch out by faith!" said one director in a confident voice; to which another director quietly replied, "Whose faith?" That simple question not only forced us to examine our own faith, but it made us turn to God in prayer and seek His direction.

D. L. Moody said, "I used to think I should close my Bible and pray for faith; but I came to see that it was in studying the Word that I was to get faith."[4]

Along with revealing God, renewing the mind, and strengthening faith, the Word of God cleanses lives: "You are already clean because of the word which I have spoken to you" (John 15:3). It is a part of the process Paul called "the renewing of your mind" because what we think determines what we are and what we do. Our Lord wants us to be beautiful, so He uses the Word to cleanse and perfect us (Eph. 5:26–27). He wants us to become more like Jesus Christ.

But the Word of God is not only cleansing water; it's also a shining light that enables us to see what's dirty and stay away from it (Ps. 119:105). Far better to *stay* clean than to *get* clean! Here's what the book of Proverbs says,

> For the commandment is a lamp,
> And the law a light;
> Reproofs of instruction are the way of life (6:23).

Over the years, I've marveled at the way the Spirit of God has used the Word to steer us clear of danger and defilement. Sometimes God used a special promise to guide us; at other times it was a loud warning; but it was the Word of God that enlightened a dark and sometimes dangerous path. I can assure you that the Word of God is indeed "a discerner of the thoughts and intents of the heart" (Heb. 4:12) and that you and I can't hide anything from God. If we come to His Word with sincere devotion and a willingness to obey, God will show us our hearts as we have never seen them before and will warn us about what may happen if we don't follow His will.

Anybody in ministry is also in a battle because the devil doesn't want to see the work of the Lord prosper. One of the enemy's favorite tactics is to question the Word of God and undermine your faith. "Has God indeed said . . . ?" is his usual approach (Gen. 3:1). Satan knows that once you start questioning God's Word, the next step is to deny God's Word; and that opens the way for him to substitute one of his own lies.

What's our defense? We must take "the sword of the Spirit, which is the word of God" (Eph. 6:17). We're like

Joshua in the promised land, fighting the enemy and claiming new territory for the Lord. The secret of victory for us is the same as it was for Joshua: "This Book of the Law shall not depart from your mouth, but you shall meditate in it day and night, that you may observe to do according to all that is written in it. For then you will make your way prosperous, and then you will have good success" (Josh. 1:8).

I suggest you discipline yourself to spend time daily in a systematic reading of God's Word. Make this "quiet time" a priority that nobody can change. I think the best time is in the morning; but all of us are different, and what is best for one might not be best for another.

As servants of the Lord, we have problems to solve, plans to make, people to help, and purposes to achieve; and we simply can't do it in our own wisdom and strength. But the Word of God equips us to live for Him and work for Him (2 Tim. 3:17). I like the way the American Standard Version of 1901 translates Luke 1:37: "For no word from God shall be void of power." When God speaks, that word has power; and when we believe that word and act on it, the power goes to work.

The better we know the Bible, the better we can know the person of God, the will of God, and how to work for God. My experience in ministry, which has privileged me to know a number of Christian leaders, and my researches into Christian biography both assure me that *Christians who live in the Word are used of God to get His work done in this world.*

Your place of service may not be a big one, but it's an important one; and God put you there because you're the right person for the job right now. He wants to work through you to get some things accomplished for His glory, and He will do it if you will "let the word of Christ dwell in you richly in all wisdom" (Col. 3:16). No matter how difficult your place of ministry might be or how discouraging the situation, adopt the attitude of Peter, and God will do wonders for you: "Master, we have toiled all night and caught nothing; nevertheless at Your word I will let down the net" (Luke 5:5).

That "nevertheless" of obedient faith makes the difference between success and failure.

You can trust in this truth: "There has not failed one word of all His good promise" (1 Kings 8:56).

23

*W*hat is God looking for?

Ezekiel 22:30 tells us that God is seeking people to "make a wall" and "stand in the gap." God is looking for workers. There are places of ministry to fill, and the angels can't take our place.

In John 4:23, Jesus states that the Father is seeking "true worshipers"; and in Luke 13:7, He informs us that the Father is also seeking fruit. These two go together, for those who commune with God bear fruit for His glory: "Without Me you can do nothing" (John 15:5).

But the statement I want to focus on is Luke 19:10: "For the Son of Man has come to seek and to save that which was lost."

God is seeking worshipers and workers and fruit bearers *because God is seeking the lost.*

While the purpose of ministry is the glory of God, one of the goals of ministry is to seek the lost and win them to faith in Jesus Christ. After all, the salvation of sinners is "to the praise of His glory" (Eph. 1:6, 12, 14). When there were only two sinners on His earth, God the Father interrupted His Sabbath rest to seek them and bring them back (Gen. 3:8–9). God the Son came all the way from heaven to seek the lost and to die for them. The Holy Spirit has been in this wicked world for nearly twenty centuries, helping the church seek and win the lost. *If reaching lost sinners is so important to God, it ought to be important to us.*

Something vanishes from our ministry when we lose our burden for lost souls. We gradually become professional Christian workers who do our job well, create no problems, but never have the blessing of seeing the gospel miracle take place in the lives of people. We lose the joy of ministry and become like the elder brother in our Lord's parable, so busy working in the field that we don't even know it when the lost have come home (Luke 15:25–32). Read Luke 15 carefully and you'll discover that the happiest people in the chapter are those involved in seeking and finding the lost.

You may be saying to yourself, "That's fine, but my ministry doesn't put me in direct contact with lost people. I'm one of those behind-the-scenes servants." That makes no difference: *every* God-given and God-empowered ministry is a part of bringing in the harvest. Some servants plow, some sow, some water, and some reap; but God gives the increase (1 Cor. 3:1–9). Whether you're cooking a dinner, cleaning the nursery, folding bulletins, or raking leaves on the church lawn, ask God to use your part of the ministry to reach lost people with the gospel.

If you're burdened for souls and sensitive to the leading of the Spirit of God, you'll be amazed at how God can use you to reach others. And even if your ministry is behind the scenes, your witness for Christ ought to be lovingly vocal and visible.

When I was in pastoral ministry, I thanked God for church workers who had a concern for the lost. They had joy and excitement in their ministry that prevented them from becoming miserable drudges (like the elder brother) and creating problems for the rest of us.

In a previous chat, I mentioned Dr. Oswald J. Smith, founder of The People's Church, Toronto, Canada, writer of many gospel songs, and a missionary statesman of international reputation. When addressing missionary conferences, Dr. Smith often reminded us, "The light that shines the farthest will shine the brightest at home." In using that metaphor, Dr. Smith was trying to demolish a serious misconception that hinders the ministry in too many churches, namely, that a big foreign missions budget compensates for a lack of evangelistic ministry at home. We all thank God for the missionary giving of our churches! It's good to win people to Christ where we don't live, but that's no substitute for winning people to Christ where we do live! As Dr. Smith's statement makes clear, the two really go together; but the shining begins at home.

So, if you have a burden to reach lost people right where you are, you'll probably have a burden to reach lost people everywhere in the world. A famous theologian once said that the church exists by mission just as fire exists by burning. The analogy is a good one and parallels Dr. Smith's metaphor. *No matter what task God has called you to do, always remember that your ministry touches a whole world if you are truly serving the Lord.* You may not see how God is using your ministry, but that's not important. You may think that your place in His vineyard is a small one, but it isn't.

Keep the big picture in mind—the vision of evangelizing a whole world for Christ—and your ministry at home will be enriched. The importance of what you do isn't measured by media interviews or press releases. As far as we know, only fifteen people in Bethany saw Mary's act of worship when she anointed the feet of Jesus—and twelve of them criticized her for it!—but Jesus said that the message of what Mary did would travel around the world! (See Mark 14:3–9; John 12:1–8.)

One of the special joys in heaven will be meeting people we never met before, people who came to Christ because of our witness and ministry, and we knew nothing about it. Another special joy will be hearing our Lord's invitation,

> Come, you blessed of My Father, inherit the kingdom prepared for you from the foundation of the world: for I was hungry and you gave Me food; I was thirsty and you gave Me drink; I was a stranger and you took Me in; I was naked and you clothed Me; I was sick and you visited Me; I was in prison and you came to Me (Matt. 25:34–36).

Like the people in the parable, we'll be shocked and ask Him, "Lord, when did we do all of that?" He will reply, "Inasmuch as you did it to one of the least of these My brethren, you did it to Me" (Matt. 25:40).

That will make ministry worth it all!

24

T he well-known American psychiatrist Karl Menninger had this to say about loyalty:

> Loyalty means not that I *am* you, or that I *agree* with everything you say or that I believe you are always right. Loyalty means that I share a common ideal with you and that regardless of minor differences we fight for it, shoulder to shoulder, confident in one another's good faith, trust, constancy, and affection.[1]

Our English word *loyal* comes from the Latin word *legere*, which means "to choose," "to pick." It also gives us the words *diligent, eligible,* and *allegiance,* all of which are good words to remember in ministry.

When Paul wrote Philippians 2:1–4, I think he had *loyalty* as well as *humility* in mind. As you read this inspired admonition, see if you get this loyalty message as I do:

Therefore if there is any consolation in Christ, if any comfort of love, if any fellowship of the Spirit, if any affection and mercy, fulfill my joy by being like-minded, having the same love, being of one accord, of one mind. Let nothing be done through selfish ambition or conceit, but in lowliness of mind let each esteem others better than himself. Let each of you look out not only for his own interests, but also for the interests of others.

There were "people problems" in the church at Philippi (4:2–3), and Paul urged the members to look beyond their friendship with Euodia and Syntyche and to remember their loyalty to the Lord. If every believer would obey Paul's admonition when people disagree in the church, we'd have fewer divisions and church splits.

When there's a difference over something in the ministry, both sides usually claim to be loyal to the Lord; and one side denounces the other side for its apostasy. It's fine to affirm our loyalty to Christ, so long as we remember that being loyal to the Lord also means *being loyal to one another.* If we are really true to the Lord, we'll be Christlike in the way we treat other people, especially those who disagree with us. That's what Paul wrote about in Philippians 2. "We ought to obey God rather than men" is a good biblical principle (Acts 5:29); but let's be sure we obey the Father the way the Son obeyed Him: "I always do those things that please Him" (John 8:29).

Practicing loyalty means first of all maintaining perspective. Many disagreements and divisions start when we focus on a minor detail and forget the big picture. I think that most Christians agree on goals of ministry but sometimes disagree on how to reach those goals. It's not the purposes of the church or the biblical principles we follow that create problems in ministry, but the procedures we use to accomplish those purposes and implement those principles. We can't compromise the commission the Lord has given us, but we can negotiate the elements of the program by which we hope to serve Him. We can't always have our way, and a willingness to give up some of our rights may lubricate the machinery.

I know of one Christian ministry that reads its "ministry purpose" at the start of every board meeting. Then the directors look at the agenda to make sure everything on it relates in some way to that purpose. If during the meeting the discussion starts to digress, somebody will say, "Focus!" and the directors will move the discussion back on track.

Another key factor in loyalty is caring about the interests of others. If I'm determined to protect and promote *only* my small corner of the field, I'm bound to create problems. I keep coming back to that quotation from Thomas Merton: "To consider persons and events and situations only in the light of their effect upon myself is to live on the doorstep of hell."

On the eve of our Lord's death, while eating with Him in the Upper Room, the twelve apostles argued over who was the greatest! It seems incredible that a hunger for recognition should possess them at the hour when their Lord was facing suffering and death. Holy places and holy occasions provide no immunity against selfishness and pride. Satan was in the Upper Room, and he has been known to attend board meetings and committee meetings, although he never answers the roll call.

Loyalty requires humility. Not the false humility of the hypocrite who baits his hook with flattery, but the true humility of the servant who says with sincerity, "What can I do to help?" God not only hates pride (Prov. 6:16–17), but He *resists* it (James 4:6; 1 Pet. 5:5). However, when we practice

117

humility, God pours out His grace; and what a difference that makes!

Loyalty must not be blind; devotion must not lack discernment. Blind loyalty could give a group of workers a dangerous "mob mentality" that makes them think they're building up the work because they're tearing down everything else. That's what Samuel Johnson meant when he defined *patriotism* as "the last refuge of a scoundrel." Plotting politicians sometimes hide behind the flag; proud Christians sometimes hide behind the cross, and to differ with them is to resist the Lord Himself.

Loyalty to the Lord and His people isn't pictured by a blender where all of us are homogenized and poured out. It's more like an army that knows where the enemy is and who the commander is, and that stands heart to heart and shoulder to shoulder, intent on one goal: victory. Paul called it "striving together for the faith of the gospel" (Phil. 1:27). True loyalty doesn't destroy your individuality; it dedicates it to a higher goal and makes you a better person because you're a part of something bigger than yourself.

"Loyalty is making yourself a part of an organization—and making that organization a part of you." I don't know who first spoke that epigram, but it makes a lot of sense. If you stop with the first part of the statement, you'll become a robot; and the organization, no matter how noble it may be, will eat you alive. But if you make the organization—the ministry—a part of yourself, so that it's something in your heart that throbs with life and challenges you, things will stay in balance. When the ministry is no longer a part of you, it may be time for you to part.

David's words of counsel to his son Solomon are significant for us today: "Know the God of your father, and serve Him with a loyal heart and with a willing mind; for the LORD searches all hearts and understands all the intent of the thoughts" (1 Chron. 28:9).

The Lord is loyal to us; He has every right to expect us to be loyal to Him and to one another.

25

You have probably learned from painful experience that the mountaintops of ministry are often accompanied by deep valleys of disappointment and discouragement. What hurts leaders the most are the failures of the people we're trying to help, people who really have every reason to succeed. Abraham must have been heartbroken over Lot's downfall; Isaac and Rebekah were deeply grieved over Esau's conduct; and Paul wept over the problems caused by people in the Corinthian church. Even our Lord once said to His disciples, "How long shall I be with you and bear with you?" (Luke 9:41). The word translated "bear" simply means "to put up with."

"To be a true minister to men," said Phillips Brooks,

> is always to accept new happiness and new distress, both of them forever deepening and entering into closer and more inseparable union with each other the more profound and

spiritual the ministry becomes. The man who gives himself to other men can never be a wholly sad man; but no more can he be a man of unclouded gladness.[1]

I suggest you read that quotation again, slowly, and let its message sink in. And the next time a Lot or an Esau or even a Judas breaks your heart, and you wonder if it's worth it all to serve the Lord, remember what Phillips Brooks said: Ministry means deeper depths of sorrow and higher heights of joy, and they often come together.

Nobody knew this fact better than Moses. No sooner did he lead the people out of Egypt than he heard them complaining that they were thirsty, and then that they were hungry. The Lord made the bitter waters sweet, He sent them the bread of angels from heaven, and He brought water out of the rock. But when Moses stayed too long on the mount with God, the people became impatient and asked Aaron to be their new leader and make them a new god. The result was the infamous golden calf and the sensual orgy that accompanied it (Exod. 32).

When he came down from the mountain, Moses exercised courageous leadership as he dealt with the people's sins; but then he had to deal with his own disappointment and sense of failure. What did he do? *He went right back to the place of duty, into the presence of God, and interceded for the very people who broke his heart!*

God made two offers to Moses: He would destroy the idolatrous Israelites, and He would make out of Moses a whole new nation. *But Moses would not use somebody else's failure to promote his own success.* He rejected both offers and asked the Lord to forgive His people and give them another chance. Neither pride nor vindictiveness ruled in

121

Moses' heart. Instead, God saw there humility and forgiveness.

When Moses was discouraged because of what his people did, he communed with God and prayed, "Please, show me Your glory" (Exod. 33:18). No matter how much we fail or our people fail, the only thing that really matters is the glory of God. The sin of Israel gave Moses the opportunity to glorify himself, but he refused to do so. One commentator proclaimed, "But the true glory and holy exultation is for a man to glory in Thee, and not in himself; to rejoice in Thy name, not in his own virtue, nor to take delight in any creature except it be for Thy sake."[2]

So, the next time people fail you and you feel like you've failed, go to the mount and ask God to show you His glory. Don't focus on yourself or the people you serve; focus on God and His glory. Before long, you'll get the perspective God wants you to have, and you'll be ready to do what He wants you to do.

Centuries later, another servant of God went to the same mountain, discouraged because the nation of Israel had failed him. It was the prophet Elijah, fresh from the victory of Mount Carmel but ready to hand in his resignation (1 Kings 19:4, 10). "It is enough!" he complained to God. "Now, LORD, take my life, for I am no better than my fathers! . . . I have been very zealous for the LORD God of hosts. . . . I alone am left."

What a contrast! Moses was heartbroken because his people deserted him and lapsed into idolatry, and Elijah was discouraged because his people didn't rally to his side when he defeated idolatry!

But Moses and Elijah handled their hurts differently. Moses saw the glory of God and, having seen that glory, found the encouragement he needed to go back and serve his people. Elijah saw only himself and what he thought was his failure; and the longer he looked at himself and talked about himself, the more he wanted to quit. *If we don't see the glory on the mountain, we'll never be able to face the discouragements in the valley.*

It's interesting that Moses and Elijah met on the Mount of Transfiguration (Matt. 17:1–8). The disappointments they had experienced in life were compensated for after death: Moses finally made it to the promised land, and Elijah finally saw the glory of God on the mount. It wasn't fire from heaven. It was glory from heaven and a voice from heaven that assured them the Father was well-pleased. Both of them saw the glory of Jesus Christ and entered into the thrill of "His decease [exodus] which He was about to accomplish at Jerusalem" (Luke 9:31). What Moses and Elijah couldn't accomplish, Jesus Christ would accomplish; but they had helped to prepare the way for His victory.

In the economy of God, suffering and glory go together. What God has joined together, you and I had better not put asunder.

26

"*I* am prepared to meet my Maker," Sir Winston Churchill told a New York news conference. "Whether my Maker is prepared for the great ordeal of meeting me is another matter."[1]

I smiled when I first read that statement, and perhaps you just did, too. But as I paused to ponder Churchill's words, I sobered up quickly, for when I meet my Maker, it will be no laughing matter: "For we must all appear before the judgment seat of Christ, that each one may receive the things done in the body, according to what he has done, whether good or bad. Knowing, therefore, the terror of the Lord, we persuade men" (2 Cor. 5:10–11).

"Serve the LORD with fear, and rejoice with trembling," admonishes Psalm 2:11. How strange that fear and trembling are linked by rejoicing, and that all three are a part of serving the Lord! Is it possible to "serve the LORD with gladness" (Ps. 100:2) and at the same time "fear the LORD, and serve

Him in truth" (1 Sam. 12:24)? Yes, it is. In fact, unless joy is balanced by godly fear, our service may not amount to very much when the fire falls at the judgment seat of Christ (1 Cor. 3:13).

The joy of the Lord grows primarily out of our *relationship* with Him, while the fear of the Lord grows out of our *responsibility* to Him. Joy and fear are neither enemies nor competitors; they're friends and allies. "In heaven, love will absorb fear," said John Henry Newman, "but in this world, fear and love must go together." Later in that same sermon, he added, "Fear is allayed by the love of Him, and our love sobered by our fear of Him."[2]

All responsibility without joy will crush a person and turn Christian service into slavery. But all joy without godly fear will make that servant shallow and immature. Jesus calls us both friends and servants (John 15:14–15). We enjoy intimacy and carry responsibility, and we must keep them in balance.

As I understand it, the judgment seat of Christ has to do with the quality of our works and whether or not they will last because they have glorified the Lord (1 Cor. 3:10–17). If we've used the wisdom of this world in building the church, everything will burn up (1 Cor. 3:18–23). But if we've used the wisdom of God in the fear of God—the gold, silver, and precious stones (Prov. 2:1–9; 3:13–18; 8:10–11)—what we've done for Him will last forever.

The judgment seat of Christ involves reckoning and rewards. Contemplating the future, *reckoning* encourages me to "serve God acceptably with reverence and godly fear" (Heb. 12:28). Thinking about the *reward* encourages me to rejoice in the Lord and serve Him with gladness. After all, God doesn't have to give us rewards. We owe everything to Him and ought to serve Him whether or not our labors are ever recognized. What grace that God not only gives us work to do and the ability to do it, but He then rewards us for what He enabled us to accomplish!

Keeping in mind that the Lord is the final judge of our service helps set us free from the fear of people and the desire to please them at the expense of pleasing God. We can't please everybody, nor should we try. Our aim should be "to walk and to please God" (1 Thess. 4:1). My experience is that God is easier to please than most people: He knows us intimately, He loves us perfectly, and therefore He can evaluate our work accurately.

Anyone who tries to serve the Lord will be criticized by both friends and enemies; and let's admit it, we probably do our own share of criticizing others. ("I'm not judging," said one critical Christian. "I'm a fruit inspector in the Lord's vineyard!") Let's not forget Paul's warning: "Therefore judge nothing before the time, until the Lord comes, who will both bring to light the hidden things of darkness and reveal the counsels of the hearts. Then each one's praise will come from God" (1 Cor. 4:5).

It's encouraging to know that God will find something to praise in each Christian's service. It's also encouraging to know that He sees our hearts—our motives—while others see only our actions. That doesn't suggest good intentions can compensate for a bad performance. But that does encourage us when we've done our best and grieve because we couldn't do better. We may not think our service will endure the fire, but He knows better.

Keeping the judgment seat of Christ in mind as you serve the Lord will discourage you from being critical of your fellow workers: "But why do you judge your brother? Or why do you show contempt for your brother? For we shall all stand before the judgment seat of Christ. . . . So then each of us shall give account of himself to God" (Rom. 14:10, 12). That's an awesome thing to contemplate: "So then each of us shall give account of himself to God."

Again, we must avoid extremes. The fact that I'll not give an account for my brothers and sisters before the Lord in the future doesn't mean I should ignore them today. If they need my help, I should help them. If I see them in danger, I must warn them. If they sin against me, I must tell them. And if they repent, I must forgive them. In other words, I should do everything I can for my brothers and sisters that will help them give a good accounting when they stand before the Lord. But I must not pass judgment on their motives or their work.

I don't know of a single well-known Christian worker in church history, ancient or contemporary, who wasn't criticized or falsely accused. Spurgeon collected the numerous critical pamphlets written against him, bound them into several volumes, and put them in his library. The people who wrote those pamphlets are forgotten, but Spurgeon's ministry goes right on. Campbell Morgan once fainted in the pulpit while refuting charges made in the American religious press that he was a "modernist." In all fairness to Dr. Morgan, I should point out that he was not a well man when that happened. His usual approach to criticism was, "It will blow over. Meanwhile, I go quietly on with my work."[3]

As God's people work together, sometimes there are disagreements and misunderstandings, even among the best of friends. Situations aren't always what they seem to be, and we may jump to conclusions and make rash judgments. It encourages me to know that our loving Lord will straighten out all these things at the judgment seat, and then all of us will praise the Lord together when we see things from His heavenly perspective.

Until then, let's follow Campbell Morgan's suggestion and get on with our work!

27

W_e all have them, and we have to accept them and learn to make the most of them. I'm talking about those bad days that every Christian worker experiences from time to time. Perhaps you didn't sleep well, you woke up with a headache, or the tele phone awakened you earlier than usual and opened your day with a crisis. If your bad day happens to be a Sunday, the difficulties are multiplied and magnified. People are depending on you, you don't want to fail them or the Lord, and yet you just don't feel like doing anything. You really feel like going back to bed!

So, what do you do?

Unless you have a serious physical problem, in which case you ought to call the doctor, the best thing to do is accept the situation, smile, take a shower, get ready for the day, and determine to do your best. If you pamper yourself every time you don't feel good, you'll end up doing less and less and eventually will do nothing.

Fortunately, acceptable Christian service isn't based on feelings; it's based on obedience. It's a matter of the will and not the feelings. When He was dying for us on the cross, our Lord was never more in the will of God; yet His body certainly didn't feel good. I think of that when my arthritis bothers me. What's arthritis compared to nails driven through your hands and feet?

Christian service that's based only on feelings will be a roller-coaster kind of experience, up one day and down the next. It will also lead to a shallow ministry that thinks more about pleasing ourselves than helping others. In the long run, service that's motivated only by our good feelings is likely to become undependable ("She doesn't *have* a headache—she *is* a headache!"), selfish ("I just don't feel like it!"), and inconsiderate ("Well, I can't help it!").

We as Christian workers, like Christian soldiers, must endure our share of hardship, or the battle may be lost (2 Tim. 2:3). Other people are depending on us, and "the greatest ability is dependability." (I don't know who first said that, but Dr. Bob Jones, Sr., used it a lot.) I would rather serve with an average worker who is reliable than a talented one who can't be depended on from one week to the next.

Make up your mind that you're going to serve God, no matter how you feel. Then you can stop wasting precious time and energy having a debate with yourself every time you don't feel good. You'd be surprised how it helps just to be committed and not have to fight the same battle over and over again.

What's next? Keeping the most vital appointment of *every* day: spending time alone with the Lord. The main thing is not how you feel as you read the Word and pray but that you listen to God, talk to God, and give yourself to Him for His special help that day. The Lord knows you better than you know yourself, but tell Him just how you feel and ask Him for the grace you'll need to do His work that day.

In my devotional time each morning, I like to pray my way through the day's schedule and turn every commitment over to the Lord. That means the day's obligations and interruptions are in His hands, and I shouldn't fret if He changes my plans. This little step of faith takes away a lot of the pressure that can be generated by a busy schedule.

On an "off day," when you go over your agenda with the Lord, see if some things on the schedule should be changed. Some activities are completely under your control, and you can cancel them or postpone them. Some obligations involve other people whose schedules may not be as flexible as yours. But if waiting a day or two will help you do a better job, provided time and other schedules are not critical factors, wisdom would dictate changing your plans and lightening the load. Of course, a lightened load today means a heavier load tomorrow or next week, but you'll be in better shape to handle it. There are no rules to guide you; you have to depend on your "spiritual instincts" as the Lord directs you.

The Lord knows about your off days long before they arrive, and He can give you the strength and motivation you need just when you need them. His grace is still sufficient, and His strength is still perfected in your weakness (2 Cor. 12:9). It's not your feelings but His faithfulness that carries you through.

Then what? Live your day, a step at a time, and do each task and meet each person as if you felt like entering the Olympics. Resist the temptation to tell others that you don't feel good. For all you know, they may feel worse; and anyway, you don't want to become toxic and spread gloom and doom. "This, too, shall pass."

I can't prove it, but I have a suspicion that much of the Lord's work is being done by men and women who don't always feel good. In fact, some of them are working under handicaps that might discourage the rest of us. Off days are not unusual for any of us, but we must not let them become excuses for pampering ourselves and creating problems for our fellow workers. Chronic physical complaints call for professional help, but occasional miseries are more nuisances than problems and ought to become servants and not masters.

If your off day turns out to be one that isn't highly structured and you can suffer courageously at home, whatever you do, don't sit around and feel sorry for yourself. Off days are also *offer* days: they offer you opportunities to catch up on routine jobs that don't demand a lot of creative concentration. I sometimes use off days to answer routine mail, index books in my sermon file, clean out the correspondence file, and even help my wife do some household task that she shouldn't handle alone. Maybe your off day is just the opportunity you've been waiting for to put photos in the album, file magazine articles, or even read the magazines that have stacked up. And it wouldn't hurt to take a nap somewhere along the line.

"He maketh me to lie down" is sometimes the reason for an off day. You may not like the interruption, but your Father knows that you've been going too long and too hard, and the time has come to rest. Busy Christian workers sometimes push themselves so much that they actually forget how to relax. If you find yourself nervous when not doing anything and always impatient to go somewhere and do something, you may be a borderline workaholic. Pay attention to God's warning; it will save you a lot of future heartache.

An off day isn't quite the same as a day off, but if your approach and attitude are right, you can make it an on day that will do both you and your ministry a lot of good.

If we can't handle the minor complaints of life heroically, how will we respond if something really serious comes our way? God might have had this idea in mind when He asked Jeremiah:

> If you have run with the footmen,
>   and they have wearied you,
> Then how can you contend with horses?
> And if in the land of peace,
> In which you trusted, they wearied you,
> Then how will you do in the floodplain of the
>   Jordan? (Jer. 12:5).

And Paul wrote something that has always encouraged me on off days: "Therefore we do not lose heart. Even though our outward man is perishing, yet the inward man is being renewed day by day" (2 Cor. 4:16).

"Day by day"—even the off days!

28

*I*f you decide to have an enemy, choose a good one because enemies are very expensive luxuries. Some anonymous wit has put it this way: "If you're nursing a grudge, expect to pay some big doctor bills." Alas, most of the price is paid on the installment plan as little by little your grudge robs you of peace and power and makes you miserable.

You can't always help *having* an enemy, but you can help *being* an enemy. Each time I read Psalm 18, I'm impressed with the way the inscription separates Saul from David's enemies. Saul considered David an enemy, but David didn't consider Saul an enemy. David couldn't stop Saul from the foolish things he did, but he could control his response to them. *If you have an enemy eating away at your heart, it's probably because you choose to have that enemy there.* You aren't responsible for the way others treat you, but you are responsible for the way you respond. Whatever ego satisfaction you get from your secret meditations about your enemy just isn't worth the wear and tear on the inner person.

I've found that my first response has to be that of prayer. Maybe the people who declared war on me don't need my prayers, *but I need to pray for them.* Jesus instructed us to love our enemies, bless them, do good to them, and pray for them (Matt. 5:44). That is a surefire remedy for protecting a heart that's in danger of being poisoned by a grudge.

"Okay," you say, "I'll pray for them; but I'm going to use one of the inspired prayers from the Psalms!" So you find one of the imprecatory psalms, join the Sons of Thunder (Mark 3:17; Luke 9:51–56), and call fire and brimstone down from heaven on the heads of your enemies.

But that isn't exactly the kind of praying Jesus was talking about in the Sermon on the Mount. We need to pray first of all for ourselves that we won't become bitter and start seeking revenge. Once we get over that hurdle, the rest will be much easier. Then we can pray for our enemies as we should and ask God to bless them with insight into His Word so they'll see their own need and turn to Him for help. We can pray for opportunities to do them good and manifest a Christlike spirit. And we also need to pray that we'll not discredit them before others but instead either say something good about them or say nothing at all: "For a bird of the air may carry your voice, and a bird in flight may tell the matter" (Eccles. 10:20).

You must keep in mind *why* the devil wants you to have enemies: if you respond to your enemy in the wrong way, the devil gains a foothold in your life. Paul's warning about giving place to the devil (Eph. 4:27) is surrounded by additional warnings about the sins that help Satan establish a beach-head: lying, unrighteous anger, corrupt speech, malice, an unforgiving spirit, to name but a few. As long as your enemies are on the outside, you're safe; but when you let them get on the inside, you're in for trouble.

If the devil sees that your enemy isn't making headway in your heart, he'll usually do one of two things: either call the whole thing off, in which case you and your enemy can be happily reconciled, or increase the pressure and try to bring you to a breaking point. If that happens, remind yourself that your battle is not with flesh and blood (your enemy) but with the invisible satanic hosts that use flesh and blood to accomplish their purposes (Eph. 6:12). Be sure you put on the whole armor of God by faith every day and use the equipment God has provided for you.

The right kind of praying ought to lead to our forgiving our enemies from the heart, even if we can't yet forgive them in person, and asking God to defuse the painful memories that could explode within and do a lot of damage. This point reminds me of a story about the late Dr. William Sangster, one of England's most effective Methodist preachers.

He was addressing Christmas cards, and a house guest was shocked to see an envelope addressed to a man who had brutally attacked Sangster eighteen months before.

"Surely you are not sending a greeting to *him*," the man said.

"Why not?" asked Sangster.

"But you remember," the guest began. "Eighteen months ago . . ."

Sangster recalled the thing the man had done to him, but he also recalled that at the time, he had resolved to put it out of his mind. "It was a thing I would remember to forget," he said; and he did.[1]

When Christians forget something, that doesn't mean they simply put it out of mind because sometimes that's difficult to do. The biblical meaning of *forget* (as in Heb. 10:17) is "not to hold it against the person and let it affect your relationship." Because He is omniscient, God can't forget anything; but He chooses not to hold our sins against us. He remembers to forget.

Sometimes personal differences are never finally settled, and we have to live with them until God decides to act. David had to endure accusation and attack from Saul until God took Saul's life on the battlefield. But even then, David didn't rejoice at the king's death. Instead, he led the nation in lamenting the deaths of Saul and Jonathan.

The pages of Christian biography are stained with the tears of Christian leaders who, for one reason or another, were unjustly attacked by people who should have been their friends and not their enemies. Many "unknown" Christian workers in churches and other ministries around the world have suffered the same way. It's hard enough to take abuse when the people of the world attack us; but when the children of God do it "in Christian love," the wounds go much deeper.

"At my first defense no one stood with me," Paul the prisoner wrote to Timothy, "but all forsook me. May it not be charged against them" (2 Tim. 4:16). And Jesus prayed from the cross, "Father, forgive them, for they do not know what they do" (Luke 23:34).

In his book *The Conduct of Life*, Ralph Waldo Emerson quotes these lines from a seventh-century Eastern poet:

He who has a thousand friends
   has not a friend to spare,
And he who has one enemy
   shall meet him everywhere.

Remember to forget.

29

*B*efore we finish chatting together, I need to say something about money. During His ministry, Jesus said a good deal about wealth, so the subject is obviously important.

I used to think that money was neutral, that the way we *use* money determined whether it was good or evil. But I've changed my mind. I'm convinced that money is basically evil and that only the blessing of God can sanctify it and make it useful in kingdom work. Jesus called wealth "unrighteous mammon" (Luke 16:9, 11) and warned that it could capture our hearts and control our wills (Matt. 6:24; Luke 16:13). Paul warned church leaders against the love of money (1 Tim. 3:3; Titus 1:7, 11), and Peter echoed the warning (1 Pet. 5:2). Recent media ministry scandals would suggest that these warnings have not always been heeded.

When Jesus used the Aramaic word *mammon*, He personified wealth and described it as a god. Some scholars think the word *mammon* comes from an Aramaic root meaning "that in which people trust." Some people trust God, some people trust wealth, and some people try to do both. Jesus was emphatic: we cannot serve both the God of heaven and the god of gold.

Why is wealth so dangerous? Because it has power and can slowly seduce us into treating it like a god. Instead of loving God with all the heart, soul, and mind, we try to love God *and* money; and before long, God loses out. The desire for money possesses the heart; thoughts of ways to get money control the mind; and before long, the will is captured, and money starts to rule the will. No wonder Paul equated "covetousness" with "idolatry" (Col. 3:5).

Money is a very satisfying substitute for God. After all, money is more tangible, and less faith is required to trust it. The Pharisees were especially guilty of trying to mix riches and religion, and Jesus told them they were wrong (Luke 16:14–15). And Paul instructed Timothy to remind the wealthy members of the church of Ephesus that "the love of money is a root of all kinds of evil" (1 Tim. 6:10). "You shall not covet" may be the last of the Ten Commandments (Exod. 20:17), but ignoring it can lead to the breaking of the other nine.

Money is the god of modern civilization, and its worship has invaded the church. It makes no difference what kind of character people have, if they are "successful"—translate that "rich and famous"—they are admired and imitated, even by Christians, who ought to know better. These celebrities show up in pulpits and are interviewed on religious radio and television. The "health and wealth" preachers have convinced millions of people that poverty is the penalty for unbelief and that the unpardonable sin is driving a used car when God can give you a stretch limousine.

Dedicated Christian workers are especially vulnerable to "money talk" because they often have to minister with what Spurgeon called "slender apparatus." It's very tempting to use the Pharisees' Law of Corban (Mark 7:9–13) and declare that, since all that we have belongs to God, we're no longer obligated to give Him tithes and offerings. Far too many Christian workers aren't faithful in their stewardship, and they're hoping nobody will find it out.

But we can't divorce money and ministry! Jesus made it clear that if God can't trust us with money, He can't trust us with the "true riches" that are so necessary for ministry (Luke 16:9–13). The worker who can't be trusted with the treasury can't be trusted with the ministry. I didn't say that—Jesus did! Here are His words: "Therefore if you have not been faithful in the unrighteous mammon, who will commit to your trust the true riches?" (Luke 16:11).

What a tragedy it is when Christian leaders sell their character just to make more money or use devious means to get people to donate more money to their work. When money takes over, character goes—and so does ministry. John Henry Jowett spoke the truth when he said, "The real measure of our wealth is how much we'd be worth if we lost all our money."[1]

Many of God's choicest servants are underpaid and over-worked, yet they count it a privilege to minister. I've met gifted surgeons on the mission field who could earn more money in a month at home than they receive in support in a year, but you don't hear them complain. Countless volunteer workers in local churches could devote that same amount of time to a part-time job or time with their families, but they're content to wait and receive their wages when their Lord returns.

Each one of us must find the economic level at which God wants us to live and be content to live there. If God gives us more than we need, we can give it away. It takes commitment and courage to challenge and defy the money myths that are fooling Christians today; but if we're going to survive in effective ministry, we have to do it. I believe that unfaithful stewardship on the part of God's people is one sin that is holding back revival in the church today.

Money is the "god of this world," and it empowers millions of people to enjoy life by living on substitutes. With money, they can buy entertainment, but they can't buy joy. They can go to the drugstore and buy sleep, but they can't buy peace. Their money will attract a lot of acquaintances but very few real friends. Wealth gains them admiration and envy but not love. It buys the best in medical services, but it can't buy health.

Yes, it's good to have the things that money can buy, *provided we don't lose the things that money can't buy.* God graciously "gives to us richly all things to enjoy" and at the same time warns us not "to trust in uncertain riches" (1 Tim. 6:17). If Christian workers can't learn to trust God for daily needs, how can we trust Him for the needs of the ministry?

Serving God means being a part of a daily miracle, and one aspect of that miracle is the way God provides for His people. "A little that a righteous man has is better than the riches of many wicked," wrote David in Psalm 37:16. Then he added his personal testimony in verse 25:

I have been young, and now am old;
Yet I have not seen the righteous forsaken,
Nor his descendants begging bread.

142

Paul would say a loud "Amen!" to that statement and then would add, "And my God shall supply all your need according to His riches in glory by Christ Jesus" (Phil. 4:19).

Can you say a loud "Amen!"to that?

30

*L*ately I've been reading "the futurists." These experts tell us what the world will be like in the decades to come and how we should prepare for it. All of them are predicting radical changes everywhere, and they're giving dire warnings that the church had better get with it. Not only is the world changing, but they tell us that change itself is changing; and the church no longer has time to play the waiting game.

Since everything else is changing, I don't doubt that change is also changing; but it doesn't disturb me too much. Not that I'm sanguine about the future, but I've read enough about the past to know that people expect the future to be ominous; and yet somehow, we have survived. One thing about change hasn't changed: it still fascinates some people, frightens others, and provides a good living for a prophetic minority.

During my lifetime, the church has been warned about the

disastrous effects on society of movies, radio, automobiles, communism, alcohol, television, "the pill," the population explosion, nuclear weapons, liberalism (theological and political), conservatism (theological and political), electing a Roman Catholic president, the cold war, pollution, ecological time bombs, abortion, sex education, ERA, the national debt, and several other threats that fell through the cracks somewhere along the line. Just about the time we thought we could breathe freely again, somebody told us to reach for our wallets and prepare for another peril.

And yet, here we are! Somehow we have survived!

Not that some of these matters aren't important and deserving of the Christian citizen's attention. But the threat of communism seems to have declined and, with it, the threat of nuclear war. They tell us that the cold war is over, although I'm not yet clear about how that will affect the future ministry of the gospel. (If I wait long enough, some evangelical "lecturer and world traveler" will write a book about it.) We survived a Roman Catholic president and even a president who didn't attend church at all. As for the national debt, many citizens are so deep in debt personally that they aren't worried about national fiscal irresponsibility.

What I'm saying is that things change, old problems fade, and new problems take their place, *but life goes on;* and you and I have but one life to live and a job to do for God before it ends. I can't do much about changing the world, but that doesn't keep me awake at night. Even the people in authority can't do much about changing the world. *But I can do something about bringing God's presence into the world in which He has put me, and that's what ministry is all about.*

Years ago I read a fable about an ant who asked a centipede, "How do you know which leg to move next?" The centipede pondered the question and replied, "I guess I've never thought about it." But the more he thought about the question, the more perplexed he became until finally he was so confused he couldn't walk at all.

We can get so wrapped up in pondering the perplexities of the future ("Which leg shall I move first?") that we fail to seize the opportunities of the present and do the work that's needed right now. Like the professional student who's dying by degrees, we're always learning how to get ready. Somebody asked the father of such a career student, "What's your son going to be when he graduates from the university?" The father replied, "An old man."

All of God's people are ministers; a few are Ministers with a capital *M*. We are either good ministers or bad ministers; but ministers we are, and as ministers we shall be judged by the Lord on the last day. On that day, it won't matter how much we knew, but what we did with what we knew. *Were we loving channels through whom the divine resources could come? Did we meet the needs of others to the glory of God?*

I'm encouraged about the future because God is in it and Jesus promised that the gates of hell would not prevail against His church. The future is our friend when Jesus is our Lord. He still goes before His sheep and prepares the way. Our job isn't to second-guess Him but to follow Him. He'll take care of the rest: "Known to God from eternity are all His works" (Acts 15:18).

Dr. Harold Lindsell once told me that he wanted the heart of an Arminian and the backbone of a Calvinist. I never had a course in theological anatomy (or anatomical theology), but I got his point; and I think Jacob Arminius and John Calvin would agree with him. It has always taken courage and compassion for God's people to minister in any age. The sovereignty of God and the love of God make an unbeatable combination for any servant of God, against which the devil has no power.

So, start ministering today, and keep ministering as long as you can. There is no discharge in this war. God has been our "dwelling place in all generations"(Ps. 90:1), and He isn't about to change and desert us. If Jesus doesn't return in our lifetimes, you and I will pass off the scene and probably be forgotten. No matter. If we've done the will of God, we've helped prepare the way for the next generation, just as others prepared the way for us.

The work goes on.

And John Wesley's dying words were right on target for today's church: "The best of all is, God is with us!"

NOTES

Chapter 5
1. A. W. W. Dale, *The Life of R. W. Dale of Birmingham* (London: Hodder and Stoughton, 1902), p. 318.
2. James L. Snyder, *In Pursuit of God: The Life of A. W. Tozer* (Camp Hill, Penn.: Christian Publications, 1991), p. 209.

Chapter 7
1. Frank S. Mead, *The Encyclopedia of Religious Quotations* (Old Tappan, N.J.: Revell, 1965), p. 391.
2. Norman Grubb, *C. T. Studd, Athlete and Pioneer* (Grand Rapids, Mich.: Zondervan, 1946), p. 129.

Chapter 8
1. G. Campbell Morgan, *The Westminster Pulpit* (London: Pickering and Inglis, n.d.), 1:243, 247.

Chapter 9
1. Andrew A. Bonar, *Memoirs and Remains of Robert Murray M'Cheyne* (London: Banner of Truth, 1966), p. 282.
2. Bonar, *Memoirs of M'Cheyne*, p. 406.
3. See my book *The Integrity Crisis* (Nashville: Oliver-Nelson, 1988) for a more detailed review of the problem and the answers.
4. Dag Hammarskjold, *Markings* (New York: Knopf, 1965), p. 122.
5. G. F. Barbour, *The Life of Alexander Whyte, D.D.* (London: Hodder and Stoughton, 1923), p. 372.

Chapter 10
1. I should have followed D. L. Moody's example. Whenever he came to a word in the Bible he couldn't pronounce, he paused to make a comment and then picked up the reading *on the other side of the troublesome word!* But I was too scared to make any comments, and I would have had to start with verse 3 of the passage.
2. Tony Castle, *The New Book of Christian Quotations* (New York: Crossroad, 1984), p. 143.

Chapter 11
1. John Buchan, *Cromwell* (London: Hodder and Stoughton, 1934), p. 368.
2. Thomas Merton, *No Man Is an Island* (New York: Harcourt Brace Jovanovich, 1983), p. 24.
3. Tony Castle, *The New Book of Christian Quotations* (New York: Crossroad, 1984), p. 194.

Chapter 12
1. Tony Castle, *The New Book of Christian Quotations* (New York: Crossroad, 1984), p. 141.
2. Castle, *New Quotations*, p. 141.
3. Charles Bridges, *An Exposition of Proverbs* (Grand Rapids, Mich.: Zondervan, 1959), p. 274.

Chapter 13
1. George H. Morrison, *The Wind on the Heath* (London: Hodder and Stoughton, 1915), p. 10.

Chapter 18
1. Charles P. Curtis and Ferris Greenslet, *The Practical Cogitator* (Boston: Houghton Mifflin, 1962), p. 148.

Chapter 19
1. *The Imitation of Christ* 1.1.3.
2. Daniel J. Boorstin, *The Image* (New York: Harper and Row, 1964), p. 163.
3. "Some Thoughts on Books and Reading," in *Man: The Dwelling Place of God* (Harrisburg, Penn.: Christian Publications 1966), p. 149.
4. Andrew A. Bonar, *Memoirs and Remains of Robert Murray M'Cheyne* (London: Banner of Truth, 1966), p. 29.
5. Henry David Thoreau, *Walden* (Princeton, N.J.: Princeton University Press, 1971), pp. 100–101, 107.

Chapter 20
1. If you're not married, you may be tempted to skip this chapter; but please don't yield to temptation. Some of what I have to say applies to every Christian worker. You might be married sooner than you expect; and while you're waiting, you can share these things with others who need them now.

Chapter 21
1. Phillips Brooks, *The Joy of Preaching* (Grand Rapids, Mich.: Kregel, 1989), p. 25. This is a new edition of Brooks's *Lectures on Preaching* given at Yale Divinity School in 1877.
2. Andrew A. Bonar, *Memoirs and Remains of Robert Murray M'Cheyne* (London: Banner of Truth, 1966), p. 282.

Chapter 22
1. Both quotations are from Tony Castle, *The New Book of Christian Quotations* (New York: Crossroad, 1984), p. 21.
2. "Break Thou the Bread of Life," words by Mary A. Lathbury.
3. A. W. Tozer, *The Knowledge of the Holy* (New York: Harper and Brothers, 1961), p. 11.
4. Stanley and Patricia Gundry, *The Wit and Wisdom of D. L. Moody* (Chicago: Moody Press, 1974), p. 40.

Chapter 24
1. Tony Castle, *The New Book of Christian Quotations* (New York: Crossroad, 1984), p. 153.

Chapter 25
1. Phillips Brooks, *The Influence of Jesus* (London: H. R. Allenson, n.d.), p. 191.
2. Thomas à Kempis, *Of the Imitation of Christ* (London: Oxford University Press, 1949), p. 183.

Chapter 26
1. *New York Times* (Supplement), Jan. 25, 1965, p. 1.
2. John Henry Newman, *Parochial and Plain Sermons* (London: Rivingtons, 1887), 1:303–4.
3. Jill Morgan, *Campbell Morgan: A Man of the Word* (Grand Rapids, Mich.: Baker, 1972), p. 372.

Chapter 28
1. Paul Sangster, *Doctor Sangster* (London: Epworth Press, 1962), p. 169.

Chapter 29
1. Tony Castle, *The New Book of Christian Quotations* (New York: Crossroad, 1984), p. 166.

Warren W. Wiersbe has pastored churches in Indiana, Kentucky, and Illinois (Chicago's historic Moody Church). He is the author of more than 100 books, including *Be Myself, The Names of Jesus,* and *So That's What a Christian Is!*